THE STRANGER IN MY RECLINER

THE STRANGER IN MY RECLINER

DOREEN M. MCGETTIGAN

TATE PUBLISHING
AND ENTERPRISES, LLC

Published by Tate Publishing & Enterprises, LLC
127 E. Trade Center Terrace | Mustang, Oklahoma 73064 USA
1.888.361.9473 | www.tatepublishing.com

Tate Publishing is committed to excellence in the publishing industry. The company reflects the philosophy established by the founders, based on Psalm 68:11,
"The Lord gave the word and great was the company of those who published it."

Book design copyright © 2016 by Tate Publishing, LLC. All rights reserved.
Cover design by Joshua Rafols
Interior design by Shieldon Alcasid
Photos by Jayne Toohey

Published in the United States of America
ISBN: 978-1-68164-370-0
Autobiography / Biography
15.10.28

Acknowledgments

To my husband John, my hero and inspiration; Tina who is forever encouraging and caring; my mother Janice and her valuable voice of reason; and my newest guardian angels, Dad and Joelle, I thank you and love you all for always being there and loving me more.

To my writing friends at Bucks County Creative Explorers and HotPenz7, I thank you for your support, your critique, and your friendship.

To those who live with mental health disorders and those that love them and to those who have survived homelessness or who are facing a frightening future, you all have my prayers and my promise for action, not just kindness and compassion.

To Heather, Joan, Jim, Jill, and Michael, thank you for tolerating me.

To my grandchildren for always making me feel like a rock star, I will forever love you more.

To Sophie, for teaching me that being nice is not the same thing as being kind because kindness is an action, for teaching me tolerance, and for helping me to realize when the right thing is the hard thing to do, we must always do the right thing anyway—always.

Contents

Prologue

Overused and Overwhelmed

The homeless people walking among us are invisible to most. We look past them, avoiding eye contact with them at all cost. I always did. Not so much purposely, it was more like subconsciously. I never wanted to look intentionally into the eyes of such vulnerable human beings. I could easily be seeing my parents, grandparents, aunts, or uncles. It could be a friend or a family member that struggles with mental illness, addiction, or chronic poverty. If I didn't look, I didn't have to *feel anything* or *do anything* for them.

I had nothing personal against homeless people. I even volunteered at a shelter a couple of times. I helped prepare meals, cleaned up the kitchen afterward, and then prepared brown-bag lunches for the adults that had jobs and for the children that went to school or day care. I enjoyed helping the kids with homework and reading to them. I even chipped in financially, along with many others, when the local newspaper *Bucks County Courier Times* requested donations so the shelter could install a new kitchen. The fund-raiser was a success, and the shelter got a new kitchen.

I met some nice, *regular* people while I was at that shelter. Many of them fell victim to a perfect storm of unfortunate circumstances, such as an illness that was followed immediately by the death or loss of a financial provider or life partner. They lost their jobs and were evicted. All of this happened in a matter of a few short months. This could happen to any of us. I could be the one pushing the shopping cart along a rickety sidewalk. That thought kept me volunteering and bringing in donations of canned and nonperishable foods to my church's quarterly hunger drives. Dropping those cans in that box always made me feel good. I was making a difference. I felt as if I earned a *free of guilt* card and was then able to move about town looking past all of those unfortunate people that walk among us. I was doing what I could do.

Giving always worked for me. Until *that* night. The night that I first met Sophie. I had no choice but to look homelessness right in its terrified eyes. I wanted to look past it, to keep walking, or to throw money and canned goods at it, but it was impossible. It was impossible because it was under my roof, sitting on my sofa, and wearing my pajamas.

Thirty-seven thousand people die homeless on the streets of America nearly every year. The number has been at least this high for years, and it is growing. This number breaks my heart. No human being should die alone on a sidewalk or in a shelter. I don't even believe animals should die alone on the streets or in a shelter. It seems at times that we do more to rescue those animals than we do our own family members. Both need rescuing.

As part of a rapidly changing demographic, baby boomers are turning sixty-five at a rate of ten thousand a day. With those numbers expected to continue until at least the year 2020, we are likely to see a dramatic spike in the already-epidemic numbers of elderly homeless people between now and then.

This should be on the first page, right up there at the top, of every policymaker's, elderly service provider's, and religious leader's agenda. We should also be discussing this at our kitchen tables among family, neighbors, and friends.

As a nation, even more as human beings, we must stop tolerating our politicians' and civic leaders' practice of throwing federal, state, local, and donated funds at referral agencies. Too many agencies do not actually provide any service other than to refer stressed-out people to one government agency after another. They are doing nothing more than passing the buck from one agency to the other. The people working in those agencies do not mean any harm. They believe wholeheartedly that they are helping. The truth is, somebody is benefitting in this situation, and unfortunately, it is not the homeless, the mentally ill, or our communities.

Our local hospital emergency rooms—urban, suburban, and rural—are being overused and overwhelmed. The police, first responders, and family members are using them as the default landing zone for those in mental health, addiction, or homeless crisis. Again, our first responders are good people with big hearts. They want to help. We need to provide them with realistic and safe solutions. Either these emergency rooms need to be equipped, staffed, and funded to be a viable solution to this epidemic or we must demand their revolving doors be closed.

If we are going to have any chance of stopping or at least containing this epidemic, we must each first examine the way we think about, react to, and treat the most vulnerable in our society. Think back, can you remember the first time you encountered a homeless or a mentally ill person? It was not a problem in America until the early 1960s. Before that time, families took responsibility for their own mentally ill, elderly, and addicted relatives. They were cared for in our own homes or placed into institutions.

The cure for homelessness will most likely be born from our collective hearts as we sit around our kitchen tables united as families, determined as communities to stop ignoring these atrocities. There has to be an answer somewhere between warehousing these human beings and continuing to put our society at large in danger for the rights of one. Because of our fear of appearing politically incorrect, we have chosen to look past these human beings and do nothing. The change must start in our hearts, continue into our homes, and spill over into our communities. We must once again become responsible for our elderly and/or mentally ill loved ones and neighbors.

That is exactly what my husband John McGettigan chose to do when he casually, like people do this every day, brought Sophie in to our home. She was an elderly woman who literally fell across his path. Because he believes that God puts people in your path for a reason, Sophie ended up on our sofa.

The woman was elderly, homeless, and mentally ill. Like most in her situation, she was frequently victimized and feared being "put away," so she never reported any of the crimes committed against her.

For me, there was absolutely nothing casual about the two and a half years John and I devoted to caring for this stranger in our home. I still have trouble understanding how we managed and why we did what we did.

Did we effect some sort of monumental change or discover the solution for the plight of the homeless? Are we holding our civic leaders and Sophie's family accountable? Why do people like us do things like bring elderly homeless women into their homes, and why is it so many others would never do such a thing?

Our profound discovery was the awareness that almost always in life, the right thing to do will predominately be the hardest thing to do. We still have to find a way to do the right thing anyway.

1

Guess Who
Is Coming for Breakfast?

My husband, John originally met Sophie at one of those twelve-step meetings. The town Prospect Park is a small working-class community just south of Philadelphia. This was not a regular meeting place for him. He was in great need that night, and it was the closest place to home with a meeting scheduled for that time of night. It was shortly after his seventeen-year-old son John died of suicide. Sophie was kind to him that night way back then. John ran into her again many times after that first meeting. He said she always had something empathetic to say to him about the loss of his son. He often gave her rides home. He never forgot the kindness she showed him or her face, and he thought about her often but he had not run into her again.

Fourteen years later, leaving that same meeting place on an unusually cold and sleeting October night, a disheveled elderly woman stumbled and fell on the sidewalk right in his path. As John reached for her hand to help lift her up, he felt something familiar.

He looked into her eyes and asked, "Are you Sophie?"

"Yes, yes, it's me, Sophie and I do remember you, John," she answered.

He gently helped her up onto her feet and then picked up what he thought were her grocery bags. After giving her a quick look over and making sure she had no injuries, he insisted on giving her a ride home. He helped her climb up into his F-150. They talked mostly about mutual acquaintances. He drove through the small towns of lower Delaware County as the windshield wipers swooshed away the sleet and rain. She asked him to drop her off at the McDonald's on Chester Pike. He told her he would take her to McDonald's, get her something to eat, and then take her home. He was of course in no mood for any of this nonsense. He was hungry, tired, and wanted to simply see her safely home. He believed there was no other choice for him, and seeing her home safely was the right thing to do in that situation.

After asking her numerous times for her address and struggling not to get frustrated with her, Sophie finally admitted to him she had no home to go to and nowhere to stay. She explained to John that she had been staying in the basement of a meeting hall. The members allowed her to stay there in exchange for cleaning the place up and making coffee for meetings.

She told him that six months earlier, a handful of members complained about her staying in the building. The members were upset because there was no shower, and they told her it wasn't sanitary. They insisted she could no longer stay there. She started sleeping in the woods behind an elementary school, not far from the twelve-step meeting place. She started to cry and told John it was so cold and wet that all she could do was start walking and hoping she would run into someone she knew, someone that could help her.

John could not believe what he was hearing. He could not comprehend how anyone could put this kind elderly woman out onto the street. He became angry and promised himself he would find out who it was that was mean enough to throw this helpless woman out onto the street. Did they even try to find her another place to stay, some place that was safe?

He was coming up on nineteen years of sobriety, and nothing about throwing a helpless elderly woman out onto the street felt like any of the twelve-step programs to him. He didn't like everyone he met in the different programs over the years, but none of the people he encountered seemed downright mean. Most of them were helpless and vulnerable themselves at one time or another and were now looking for a way to pay it forward, a way to help those still struggling with their addictions.

John called to ask me if he could bring a woman home for the night. Yeah, not the thing you expect your husband to call and request of you. I had no idea what to think or what to expect, but once he explained the situation, of course I said yes. I didn't feel as though there was any choice.

Immediately after I said yes to him, I was stricken with panic. Why was this woman homeless? My first thought was she is mentally ill. Of course she was. Aren't all homeless people mentally ill? Perhaps she was schizophrenic or some sort of sociopath. Then I thought she was probably a drug addict and an alcoholic. Of course, she was addicted in some way. He met her at one of those meetings. She was most likely all of the above. She had to be, I decided. Honestly, I had no idea what to expect. Nervously, I started walking around the house, picking things up, rearranging shelves, and dusting. I spritzed the furniture and throw rugs with Fabreeze. I think I am seriously addicted to that stuff. I continued walking around in a numb sort of state of panic, talking to myself. I felt guilty for assuming the worst about this woman, as well as anyone who found themselves homeless. The past few years were financially devastating for far too many good, hardworking people.

I was so tired. I worked as a companion for an elderly woman. A woman that was very ill. I just finished a twelve-hour shift with her. I was in no mood to stay up making small talk with and playing host for someone I did not know, let alone some out-of-her-mind, homeless, alcoholic woman.

I still wasn't completely sold on any of those twelve-step recovery programs. The drug addicts and alcoholics I had come across in my life and some unfortunately in my own family either went to jail, died, or seemed to disappear into the woodwork. I never knew of anyone that truly "recovered." Some would stop using for a while, but almost all of them picked up drugs or alcohol again. What seemed so crazy to me was the fact that some of them picked up their old vices at seemingly happy times in their lives. I honestly believed addiction was basically a life sentence—a terminal, hopeless illness.

That was until I met John. It was a huge red flag when I first met him. He told me he was a recovering alcoholic and drug addict on our first date. Since then, the man proved to me that people that are willing to change are capable of change. It took me a while to understand why after nineteen years, he still went to those meetings. For him, it was not only about giving it away to those in need but also a reminder of how he himself was just one sip from death. He was convinced that if he ever took that one drink, he would never be able to stop himself.

I was always more of an enabler. I was never much of a drinker, although I did and still do enjoy a glass of wine with dinner every now and then. As far as drugs, I was never a fan of them, and I honestly thought poorly of anyone that grew up and was still indulging in them.

John helped me to understand that it truly was a disease, one with no cure. The only hope is treatment that can help to manage the symptoms. My argument always is, if you have a disease, you can choose to get treatment or you can die. I did not understand why alcoholics and drug addicts so often fight getting treatment. I don't know of many people with cancer that decide they would rather die of the disease than go through the grueling hard work it would take them to get well or at least into remission. Even the sickest, terminal patients will endure agonizing treatments for the opportunity of a few extra months with their loved ones. I wondered if the addicts' inability to make the right choices and seek treatment meant that alcoholics and drug addicts underneath their addictions also suffered from some form of mental illness or mental health disorder. I was convinced that was the case. Stopping the drinking and/or drugs was just the first step. These patients need counseling and probably psychological help as well.

When Sophie walked through my front door that night, I could not believe my eyes. She was a frail, filthy, and hunched-over eighty-year-old woman. I wondered if she had bugs. I'm OCD (obsessive-compulsive disorder) like that. I told her to sit on the sofa, while the whole time in my mind, I was making it all better for me by imagining myself throwing that big red sofa away and buying a nice, clean new one. Maybe an L-shaped brown microfiber one this time.

I made her a hot cup of tea. After noticing she had no teeth and wondering what in the world could have happened to them, I made her a scrambled egg. While she ate her eggs and talked with John about people they might mutually know, I went upstairs and prepared her a warm bubble bath. I gave her my favorite silk pajamas, clean underwear, a warm fluffy pair of socks, and a thick robe. The pajamas were a gift from my kids. They gave them to me when I was in the hospital for treatment of a bad allergic reaction to a vitamin supplement made from shellfish. I was certain they would understand why I had to give them to Sophie.

While she was in the bathroom having her bath, I made up the big red sofa with our softest six-hundred-thread-count guest sheets, our best pillows, and a warm cotton blanket. I wanted her to feel safe, warm, and comfortable. Whatever the reason for her plight, no one should be sleeping on the ground in this crazy weather. John thanked me for allowing him to bring Sophie into our home. He gave me a hug and promised me everything would be okay. He sensed my growing discomfort, so he hugged me again. I love that he has the ability to sense my feelings.

I wanted to ask her a thousand questions. Do you have a family? Were you ever married? Do you have children? How did you get yourself into this situation? Are you still drinking? That was the big one. That would be bad. I decided not to ask too many questions that night. I did ask her where the woods were located, the ones she had been sleeping in, and she told me they were alongside MacDade Boulevard. MacDade Boulevard is the main thoroughfare connecting a dozen or so small towns in Delaware County, leading to Philadelphia. She also told us that night she was attacked and robbed often.

Talk about a soft target, and for what, a few coins at the most. I felt so sorry for her and such anger for those unknown scumbags that would hurt her. I wanted to know more but decided I would ask her another time. I thought she must be physically and mentally exhausted. I thought she might be embarrassed too. I would be horrified if I found myself with nowhere to go and I had to wear a stranger's underwear, their clothes, and sleep on their sofa. I would also be scared to death if I had no choice but to trust in the sincerity and saneness of strangers. I did not want to think about that stuff anymore.

She seemed to trust in John completely. With me, she was completely unsure. She most likely sensed my fear and disapproval. I had the feeling there was so much more to her story. How could there not be more. How do you get to be eighty years old and not have met at least one person that loved or at least cared enough about you to take you in from the cold? What possibly could have happened to her, what sin or crime did she commit that would force her to have no choice in the world but to trust complete strangers over family or friends? Wondering about those possible sins and crimes scared me to my core.

My husband, on the other hand, is the least judgmental person I know. He is trusting to a frustrating fault. I admired his compassion and knew in my heart that keeping her safe and warm on this cold, wet night was the right thing to do no matter how she came to be in this situation.

Even if it was wrong of me, I could not help wondering why I had to be the one to do *that* particular right thing on *that* particular night.

We made sure she had everything she could possibly ever need during the night. I poured a glass of ice water and placed it on the end table beside the red sofa. I put a few magazines on the coffee table. We asked if she would like to watch some TV. She said she would like that. I found an old movie on AMC, *Duel in the Sun*, and I was thrilled to see the light in her eyes.

"I love Joe Cotten," she said, smiling. "He is my favorite actor."

I had no idea who Joe Cotten was, but I did notice that Gregory Peck and Lionel Barrymore were in the film. I wished I wasn't so tired. I wouldn't have minded watching it with her if John would have stayed up to watch it too. Instead, John and I went to bed. I imagined that it must have been a long time since she was able to watch and enjoy a good movie. It felt good to do that for her.

Turning the latch on my bedroom doorknob ever so slowly so she wouldn't hear the click, I locked our bedroom door and tiptoed over to our bed. Yes, I admit it. I was scared. I had visions of this crazy bag lady stabbing us in our sleep, robbing us, or having her homeless gaggle of friends coming into our house to party through the night. I shuddered at the thought of the endless horrific things they could do to us. I tossed and turned all night. I tried to imagine how anyone could let an eighty-year-old woman become homeless and then reverted to what could she have possibly done to find herself in this situation.

The truth is, I wanted her and the sting of the slap-in-the-face reality of her situation to go away. I felt guilty that I felt that way.

I rolled over and flipped my pillow again, hoping to find a small patch of cold on the other side. Memories flooded my mind. I had a history with homeless people, and it was not always good. I took in a homeless woman with a six-week-old infant when I was a young divorced mom. My kids and I fell in love with the baby. Danielle lived with us whenever her mother was in prison, which was several times over an eight-year period. The mother emotionally blackmailed and sometimes even terrorized my family for years. A priest told me that sometimes we have to make the choice to hurt one to save many others. I hated the sound of that advice. We did not want to, but we sent that little girl to live with her father and her older sister in Minnesota. It wasn't fair of us to keep her from knowing her family. Our hearts are still broken.

I took in a young man that worked for me when I managed a Pizza Hut restaurant. He was a homeless drifter, a musician. I found out he smoked pot in front of my young daughters and their friends. I was horrified, hurt, and furious.

Another time, I took in a childhood friend of my sister's. The woman had two young children, and they were living in an abusive situation. Her husband had no idea I existed, so they would be safe and able to get a head start on a new life. It was a struggle for her and her children.

I admired her for finding the strength to leave him and for loving her children so much that she gave up everything to keep them safe. I was thrilled when she moved on, fell in love, and remarried a gentle man.

I do not regret helping any of those people, but now that I am older and look back, I realize what dangerous situations I put my family, my own children, in at times. That woman's abusive husband could have found her at my house and killed us all. That little girl's mother was jailed several times for terroristic threats. I shudder when I imagine what could have happened. I do not mean to be over dramatic, but you only have to watch the Lifetime Movie Network to know it can and unfortunately does happen when you least expect it.

I seem to constantly be asking myself if the fear I developed with age is a good-enough reason to do nothing. Of course, the answer is no. It is not a good reason. Eliminating the fear and replacing it with knowledge is a good start. It is always easier to open a door if you have a reasonable expectation of what is waiting for you on the other side of that door.

I flipped my pillow again and rolled onto my side. Why didn't I leave some cookies, crackers, or chips out for Sophie? I wondered if she was still hungry. There was no chance I was going downstairs to find out. John was sound asleep.

What do you do in those situations where there is no way to know what is behind that door? You can choose to stay stuck, or you can dig deep for the faith and courage to open that door. I would rather have stayed stuck in my safe, comfortable world that night, secure in the fact that I had done enough good deeds in this lifetime. John, however, on that night needed me to walk through that door with him.

He was grieving the loss of his mother. She passed away six months prior to him finding Sophie on that sidewalk. John and I met and married shortly before his mother became ill. Kathleen was the first elderly person I ever lived with, and the first elderly person I ever provided with hands-on care. Honestly, ever since I was a small child, I was afraid of older people. We had a few cranky neighbors when I was a kid. The older kids would tell us stories about being captured by these creepy old people and kept chained in their smelly basements.

I always adored my own grandmother, except for the times when she was yelling at my poor grandfather. While I was growing up in the Somerton section of Northeast Philadelphia, she lived just a few blocks from our house. We saw her every day. As I got older, I would drive her to doctor appointments, take her to the grocery store, clean for her, or just sit and visit. Back then, she never seemed old to me. When my younger brother was murdered, Grandmom started to look tired to me. Her grief sapped her energy and her health. When she did become sick, she went downhill and passed away quickly. My grandfather got sick years before and took his own life before he had the chance to grow old.

For the first time in our young marriage, John and I were living alone. We were just getting used to our newly found freedom. We discussed traveling, home renovation projects, and retiring at the seashore. We discovered our living room. For two years, the room was a campground for John's sisters and nieces who thankfully were there to help care for his mother. That is the way it is supposed to be. Families are supposed to come together and come up with a workable solution to provide care for their elderly loved ones. It is one of those times in life that you must put your own needs and feelings aside and work as a team, a family unit.

I enjoyed the chaos of so many people coming in and out of the house. That was what I was used too. The situation helped me to be less homesick. When we married, I moved in to his home. He lived in another county, on the other side of Philadelphia. I was used to seeing my kids and grandkids every single day. When the house was quiet, I missed them terribly.

What a long night that first night with Sophie turned out to be. As I walked downstairs in the morning, I was hoping it had all been a long dream. There was no such luck. There she was, sitting on the end of the big red sofa. She was awake and as real as my freezing feet on the cold floor. She was dressed in her own dirty old clothes. Those ripped plastic grocery bags that were full of I have no idea what were at her feet. We originally thought they held some sort of groceries, but, no, they definitely did not hold groceries. She clutched a filthy, overstuffed pocketbook with a broken strap to her chest. Her head was down; she was staring at the floor. She looked so fragile. I noticed the pajamas, underwear, and those fluffy socks I gave her folded neatly beside her. My first thought was, not believing she put her dirty underwear back on her nice, clean body. I cringed. My second thought was, she must have been a beautiful woman. Her hair was pure white, not at all that dingy gray most of us are stuck with. It was so long and wavy. Most of the older women that I knew wore their hair short. I wondered if she ever colored it. It was so beautiful this morning compared to the filthy, stringy mess it had been last night before her bath.

I made her a cup of hot tea and some instant apples and cinnamon oatmeal for breakfast. Oatmeal is not one of my favorites, but I love the way the flavored ones smell. She seemed thrilled when I handed her a banana. It didn't seem like the right time to ask where her teeth were. I hoped I never had the opportunity to ask.

I wanted to tell her it was okay to stay here in our nice warm house for the day. I also did not want to tell her she could stay here in our nice, clean warm house. John and I were both working from 9:00 a.m. until 9:00 p.m. I could not help but think it was possible she could completely clean out our house in twelve hours and God forbid, let all kinds of other "scary" people know where we live. Again, I felt guilty for feeling and thinking that way, but it is what I thought. Sort of the same way I always felt guilty for being afraid to be in an elevator alone with a stranger or when someone follows me too close in a parking lot or on a sidewalk at night. It is a natural instinct, that *uh-oh* warning feeling most women are blessed with. I don't understand why we are always apologizing for it.

2

Nobody Answered

John agreed to drop Sophie off at *her* McDonald's that morning. I think it is funny how in our area we claim fast-food restaurants, convenience stores, and other establishments as *my* McDonald's or *my* Wawa. I suppose it is because there seems to be one in every neighborhood. Maybe people elsewhere in the country do that too, I'm not sure. It seems odd to me.

John told Sophie he would come by the restaurant at nine thirty that night, and if she were still there, he would bring her home with him again. She smiled and gathered up her grocery bags. We told her she could leave what she did not need for the day at our house. He assured her it would be completely safe, but she flatly refused. I could not even imagine what was in those bags. I wanted to dump them and reorganize the contents and put whatever they held into the two large canvas bags with strong handles that I had under my kitchen sink. I wanted to do it for her as much as to satisfy my own OCD.

She said, "No, thank you."

John shot a begging *I hope it's okay with you* glance my way. Of course, she could spend the night with us—again. It was freezing outside, and the forecast seemed to get worse with each passing hour. What else would I say especially in front of Sophie? I secretly hoped she would not be there when John showed up at the McDonald's later that night. I hoped one of her family members or, better yet, a group of her family members would find her and take her home with them, where she belonged. I hoped she wasn't homeless, and it was all a big misunderstanding. Maybe she became confused and wandered away from them and only imagined she slept in the woods for six months. That was a safe, guilt-free kind of thought. I prayed for it to be reality.

John must have sensed my discomfort. He laughed at me the night before when I locked our bedroom door. He told me she would never hurt anyone, especially not us. My husband tried to convince me she crossed his path again for a reason. He reminded me how kind she was to him all those years ago when his life was shattered. I wondered if I should and how I could put my foot down and say no, because there was no way I wanted her in our house again that night. I could argue and say to him that there were many people I met in my life "one night" that were nice to me. That did not mean we were lifelong friends and I needed to rescue them all, did it?

At work that day, I made a mental list of places in our county that I could contact to get some services for Sophie. In Delaware County, Pennsylvania, where we live, there is an organization that assists the aging called County Office of Services for the Aging, or COSA. I also put public assistance on the list, social security, and our congressional representative at the time who was Joe Sestak. I also listed Catholic Social Services.

The next day was my regular scheduled day off, so I decided if Sophie did come home with John, I would spend the entire day searching for, finding, and then getting her settled into a new place. It was a way to do some good, I thought. I assumed there would be numerous emergency housing assistance programs for situations like Sophie's. I sat back and enjoyed decorating her new apartment in my mind. I was thinking that this could turn out to be fun. We could give her that big red sofa, I thought. I created a list, an inventory of no-longer-needed household items in my mind. I had so much to donate to that great cause.

I usually spent the days I had off either writing, visiting my kids, and, of course, doing the usual cooking, cleaning, laundry, and grocery shopping. Helping Sophie would be a nice diversion. I missed the volunteer work I used to do with the Network of Victim Assistance, or NOVA, when I lived in Bucks County, Pennsylvania. That organization literally saved my life when my younger brother David was murdered during a random road rage attack.

When I suddenly realized John would be working the next day from nine o'clock in the morning until nine o'clock at night, I felt like an idiot. I would be completely alone with a stranger who could very well be a vicious killer, or not.

I tried to shake off my all-consuming negative thoughts and fears. I kept repeating to myself, "The right thing to do is not always the easiest thing to do." I kept saying it, but it did not help my growing anxiety.

I arrived home at nine twenty that night. John was not there. He called earlier to remind me he was going to drive by the McDonald's on his way home to look for Sophie. It was not likely I could ever forget about Sophie, let alone forget she may be sleeping on our sofa again that night.

I cleaned the muddy coffee grounds from the coffee pot, rinsed it out, and refilled it with fresh coffee grounds and water for the morning. I started to empty the dishwasher. Trying to work quickly, I picked up two coffee mugs at once. Water had pooled on the bottoms of the mugs. When I picked them up, the water dripped all over the front of my shirt. I ran upstairs to change. The house was so quiet. I went back downstairs into the living room, and I turned on the television. Listening to the news or a random talk show was comforting to me when I was home alone. I am the oldest of five kids. While I was growing up, our house was always noisy and chaotic. By the time I was twenty-two years old, I had my own house full of kids and chaos. I still had trouble adjusting to the stillness and the quiet in this house since John's mother passed away.

John called at ten o'clock to tell me Sophie was not at the McDonald's. I could actually feel the huge sigh of relief building up in my body. Thank you, God, I thought. I let go of most of my panic with a long sigh but reserved some of that panic deep down in my gut. She possibly went somewhere else for the night or her family found her. Maybe someone called the authorities and she was picked up and taken to some sort of agency that could help her.

John told me he was going to drive around a bit to see if maybe she was walking toward the restaurant. He sounded tired, and I could tell that he was frustrated. He found her wandering aimlessly on the sidewalk alongside Chester Pike. She mixed up the time and thought John had forgotten her. She was upset.

I was relieved to hear she was okay, but I also felt a bit put out at the same time.

He told me they would be home shortly. I took a deep breath as I put on the teakettle and made up the big red sofa again. I laid out the silk pajamas, clean underwear, a fresh pair of warm socks, and the robe. I gathered up my purse and some other personal items and took them upstairs. There was no harm in being cautious. I started the bath water, added some bubbles, and sat there on the edge of the tub wondering what tomorrow would be like. I was tired. I tried to focus on how good I would feel when this poor woman was in her own safe place. I thought about how good she would feel to have a place of her very own where she could comfortably spend what would most likely be the last few years of her life.

We could visit her. I would bring her the occasional meal, and I could drive her to the store for groceries. John could pick her up and take her to meetings with him. We could pick her up a collection of Joe Cotten movies as a housewarming gift.

Sophie took a nice warm bath, we ate, and John and I said good night to her. I quietly locked the bedroom door again and asked John to please not laugh at me and to relock it before he left for work in the morning. I was afraid of her, and who wouldn't be? I also wanted to sleep in just a bit later than usual. I did not sleep well the night before. John asked what my plans were for the next day. I told him I was going to start with phoning the public assistance office, and I would go on making calls from there. He thanked me for being kind to Sophie. I felt guilty because I wasn't sure if some of my thoughts were as kind as my actions were. They should have been. I needed to work on that.

I made Sophie and I some eggs and put some bread in the toaster. I knew it would get stuck and burn if I didn't keep my eye on it. As usual, I allowed myself to get distracted. The burning smell was awful, and instead of scraping the blackness off the toast, I just tossed it into the trash can and put two fresh pieces of bread in the toaster. This time, after a minute, I forced the lever on the toaster and popped the toast onto a plate.

Promptly at 9:00 a.m., I called the public assistance office in Upper Darby. Nobody answered the phone. It just rang and rang. I patiently waited for an answering machine to click on, but none ever did. I don't know about you, but when I know I am dealing with an organization run by your tax dollars and mine and nobody answers the phone, it makes me angry. It most likely isn't the employees' fault. In most cases, it is the incompetent management. If these government agencies were run like for profit business, they would run a lot smoother and efficiently. I'm also quite sure the fraud could be practically eliminated. Why can't we make that happen? That particular agency, the one in Darby, PA, had been in the news recently. Apparently, a lot of fraud was being committed, especially with SNAP (the food stamp) program.

The owner of a Darby Borough food market pleaded guilty to food stamp fraud. She was illegally exchanging food stamps for cash.

The government estimated the fraud in that case cost taxpayers more than $295,000 from 2008 through 2010.

Federal authorities became suspicious when the owner requested payments well above the estimated $80,000 in sales she put on her application. She requested reimbursements of $120,346 in 2009, $211,766 in 2010, and $270,317 in 2011 according to the indictment.

An undercover investigation showed the storeowner was exchanging cash for food stamp benefits by generating phony transaction amounts in varying dollar amounts and then giving the customer approximately 60 percent of the transaction amount in cash, the indictment said. This crime is happening all over the country in small towns, large towns, big cities, basically everywhere, and it is literally taking food out of children's mouths and putting illegal drugs into the mouths and arms of addicts and thugs.

In cases like this one, the cost of prosecution is extremely high, and the immediate return on the investment is practically nonexistent. This leaves district attorneys and attorney generals little incentive to prosecute.

Just thinking about that fraud happening in that tiny borough and knowing that it is only the tip of the iceberg and it is happening in tiny towns and big cities all across the United States makes me angry. I cannot help but be angry at some of the people in those towns that make it all about money. Unfortunately, more money doesn't stop greed, and it certainly doesn't stop drug addiction and criminal mentality issues.

I redialed every five minutes, and finally, forty-five minutes later, a woman answered and told me I needed to call the assistance office in Chester. At least this office was closer to where we lived. It would be easier if we had to show up in person, although I was hoping they wouldn't require us to do so. Some parts of Chester are extremely dangerous, and I had no idea where those areas where. I dialed the number.

I feel so bad for the good people living there, trying to raise families among the dangerous chaos. It was not an area I wanted to bring an elderly woman, especially by myself. Again, the phone rang and rang and rang. I tried again fifteen minutes later. No one answered again. My nerves couldn't take much more, so I moved on to Catholic Social Services. Sister Marie had visited John's mother a few times. She would come by for a cup of tea. She said she would come out to see Sophie and me the following Thursday, which was my next day off. This day was not feeling productive at all, and I was feeling frustrated.

I decided to skip the phone calls for a while and move on to e-mails. I went upstairs to my office to look up the e-mail address for our congressman's office. I did a little campaigning for him, so I was hoping he would come through for Sophie. The e-mail would be easier, I thought as I typed the story of how Sophie came to be in our home and a list of the agencies I was planning to contact on her behalf. I hit send.

He is the answer to Sophie's dilemma, I thought.

Congressional representatives are supposed to be there to assist their constituents and to make sure their districts have the best assistance programs available. They should also be monitoring the programs for fraud and making sure the results are positive.

I looked for a COSA Web site. I was only able to find the phone number. I explained Sophie's situation, and the woman on the other end of the phone said someone would need to get back to me. It was lunchtime. I went downstairs and opened a can of tuna. I carefully put the lid back over the top and squeezed the oily, nasty water out of the can and into the sink, trying not to splash it all over me. I didn't put anything crunchy like celery, onions, or, my favorite, black olives into the tuna fish because I didn't think Sophie would be able to chew it without teeth. I wondered again what happened to her teeth. How would I bring up that conversation? I put our sandwiches on plates and brought them into the living room. I turned on *The Young and the Restless*. I started watching the show more than thirty years ago when I was home on maternity leave with my youngest daughter. It wasn't often I was able to actually sit down and watch it in real time. I usually recorded it and watched it at night after John fell asleep.

Sophie asked the most annoying questions throughout the entire show. I patiently answered each one and also tried to give her the short version of each character's backstory. During the commercials, I snuck in a few questions of my own. I asked her where she lived before she became homeless. She told me a good friend of hers was diagnosed with cancer and needed help and care. Sophie offered to move in with the woman and to take care of her while she underwent her treatments. She became the primary caregiver of this woman for a few years up until the time the woman passed away. Shortly after the woman died, in fact only three days after, Sophie came home and found all of her belongings inside plastic grocery bags on the sidewalk. The dead woman's children were not around while their mother was sick and needed their help, but they were there to immediately sell her house so they could collect on her death.

What a bunch of brats, I thought. Sophie said they would not even let her back into the house to call someone for help. They also would not give Sophie the details of any service that was being planned for their mother. Sophie was devastated and suspected they were not even going to plan a service. Sophie believed they had her friend cremated.

I tried to imagine what reason those adult kids had for being so mean to Sophie. Why were they dishonoring the memory of their mother? Were they hurting Sophie to get back at their mother for some reason, or had Sophie done something to them?

Sophie told me that afternoon she had a monthly income. She said she received social security and a small pension but had no savings. She was unable to pay a first and last months' rent plus a security deposit on an apartment at that time. She went on to tell me she stayed with some of her friends here and there when she could, but none of them offered her permanent residency.

Sophie also told me she should have been receiving a higher pension, but a woman she worked with for many years stole the credit for sales that she actually made. I had no idea what that meant or even if I believed it. What I did know was Sophie believed it to be true and it upset her.

Sophie told me she had a son named Frankie. Frankie met an older woman who had plastic surgery to make herself look so much younger that Frankie would want to be with her. They had a daughter together.

"She is a sweet little girl and so pretty." Sophie smiled proudly.

I was not able to immediately come up with a follow-up question for that one. How much of that story was real, I wondered.

She spoke fondly of this son. "He's a good boy," she said over and again.

All I could come up with to ask her was, "Where does he live?"

She said he went to California with that old woman.

That is disappointing, I thought.

Could we ever get her to California to be with this son?

She went on to tell me she had a daughter she called Peaches. She said Peaches stole her boyfriend and her money and moved to North Carolina with that person. The daughter was supposed to go to North Carolina to buy a home with an in-law suite or a duplex and then come back for her mother.

My head was spinning. I had to say, "She stole your man, and then you gave her your money, and you were planning to go live with them?"

Suddenly, *The Young and the Restless* storylines became much more believable, less shocking. I asked her if Peaches had any children. Sophie told me she did but made it more than obvious she did not want to discuss them or their whereabouts with me. I was trying to do the math in my head. I was trying to figure out the possible ages of these supposed children and grandchildren. Sophie was eighty, so her kids most likely were in their late fifties or early sixties. She could feasibly have thirty- or even forty-year-old grandchildren. Possibly even a whole slew of great-grandchildren. Where were they now?

She also had a son named Billy that lived in the area. My heart pounded out a few extra hopeful beats. I asked why she did not live with him. Sophie said Billy's wife hated her. That answer made my head spin. I thought Billy should have dumped his wife and took care of his mother. I know there were always two sides to a story, and I had no idea what Billy's story was, but whatever the story was, it seemed cruel to me to allow your elderly mother to sleep in the woods. What kind of woman that loves her husband lets his elderly mother not only sleep outside in the cold but also sleep on the hard ground. Most definitely, a woman I never wanted to know.

My head continued to spin, so I let up on the questions for that day. It was all too much for me to process at one time. I went back to obsessively dialing the phone I was willing, wishing, and hoping some government employee would eventually answer. At three forty-five in the afternoon, an actual person finally answered the phone at the assistance office in Chester. The woman who answered the phone was very pleasant. She made it difficult for me to continue feeling put out and frustrated with the time it took for her to answer. I wanted to vent, but she was too nice. She told me Sophie already existed in their system and even had a caseworker. His name was Mr. White. She offered to connect me to his extension. I thanked her. He did not answer, but thankfully, someone *finally* had voice mail, so I left him a message.

That day turned out to be a total waste of my time. The only hope I had was for the organizations I contacted to get back to me quickly. It was looking like Sophie would be going back to her McDonald's again the next day.

Wanting to move on, I asked Sophie what her favorite things to eat were. She said she loved canned peas and she hated chili. That was all I got out of her. I wondered if she heard John and me discussing possibly making a big pot of chili that week. Of course, she heard us talking. I shivered a little. What a creepy feeling that thought caused. I prepared a shopping list, gathered my coupons, and went to the store.

I was more than uncomfortable leaving her alone in our home. I shopped quickly. When I got back to the house, Sophie was still sitting in the same place she was sitting in when I left. She did not move. That made me sad. I was also sad because I hated leaving her alone in our home.

I wondered how is it possible to feel so annoyed at this *person*, this total stranger that was here sitting on my sofa, invading my personal time and space, and at the same time just want to annihilate anyone—and everyone—involved in allowing this fragile elderly woman to be left all alone out here in this unsafe big world. I just wanted to hug her and tell her not to worry and that we would always take care of her. I did not do that, but I thought it and I wanted to do it. I was just scared.

I went into Kathleen's room. We had not yet made a decision on what to do with this room. My husband would have been happy to leave it as was forever. He would like to turn it into a shrine. He missed his mother so much. She was always the one person in his life who understood who he was and accepted him for him. I missed her too. She made me feel so welcome in her home and in her life. She told me she knew how much I loved John and she knew I would be there for him.

One night after she had a nightmare, I promised her I would always be there for John. I would always encourage him and love him for who he was. She asked me to remind him often to do everything in moderation. That thought made me smile. She was so right. That man needs constant reminding that moderation is a good thing. I wondered what she would have thought of him bringing Sophie home. She would no doubt be proud of him for his acts of kindness.

I opened the closet and went through what was left of her clothing. I picked out two outfits, a pair of pajamas and a sweater. I felt guilty for feeling so sad, for missing my mother-in-law so much. I only knew her for such a short time. John and his sisters had her for their entire lives. Their hearts were and continue to be broken.

I remembered another night when Kathleen had a nightmare. "Sundowners" is the unofficial definition for these episodes. I was not happy that night, to say the least. I was exhausted, emotionally drained, physically tired, and felt very sorry for myself. I sat in the chair beside Kathleen's bed and reached for her hand. I told her I would sit with her until she went back to sleep. We always left the television on for her so she would not feel alone. That always worked for me too. I looked up at the screen, and she had one of the religious channels on. Oh, jeez, I thought. Do not get me wrong, I am a Christian woman. I tried to be the best person I could be—a good example, loving and kind, and all of that religious stuff. I just did not want to listen to some old priest at that moment on that night.

"Turn it up a little," she quietly asked.

After a quick scan for the remote control, which was chronically lost in that room, I got up and turned the volume up manually.

"Hey, you," the priest said. I sat back down and took Kathleen's hand again. "Yes, you. How dare you complain about taking care of your elderly family members? How dare you be so selfish?" I kept blinking my eyes trying to wake up because that sure did feel like a dream. This old priest was talking directly to me, and it was creeping me out big time. He went on to say, "When in your life will you ever be so close to someone who is about to leave for the other side, perhaps even go to heaven?"

That priest on that night affected me profoundly. He was so right. I was overcome with a blessed feeling. I suddenly felt honored to be keeping this special woman company right before she went on to have tea with the angels in the gardens of heaven. I had a twinge of that feeling again on that day as I stood at her closet, touching her clothing. What would she think of Sophie? Would she have been proud of her son or frightened as I was? I wondered if Sophie was going to heaven one day soon. John was convinced she was a good-hearted person. I wasn't completely convinced she was heavenly material.

I went upstairs into another one of our spare bedrooms and went through some of my own clothes. I picked out two more outfits, a robe, and some warm socks. I took them downstairs and told Sophie to go through them and decide if she would ever wear the stuff. I folded everything and put it on the table in Kathleen's room and told Sophie to feel free to get dressed in there. I put a toothbrush, a few fresh towels, and some other toiletries in Kathleen's bathroom and told Sophie to feel free to use that bathroom.

I went back upstairs into my office and tried to write. I wanted to finish a chunk of edits on my first book. It was hard to concentrate. I used to read whatever I was writing to Kathleen. I also read most of the rejection letters I received to her.

"Send it to the next one on your list right away," she would tell me. "They have no idea what they are missing."

I smiled again at the memory of her encouraging words. She may have only been in my life for a couple of years, but I could not have ordered a more supportive mother-in-law and friend. It was hard after her death to get back into some sort of writing groove.

It was a definitely a struggle that day to concentrate, but I managed to get through ten pages. I played Scrabble Blast until the guilt of leaving Sophie alone downstairs reached my last nerve. I went downstairs to cook dinner and watch the news with her. We were both anxious for John to get home from work.

3

Domestic Politics

The following day, I received a response to my e-mail from our congressman's office. The woman in charge of responding to the congressman's e-mails sent me a list of places I should contact for assistance. As I looked over the list, I felt flat-out dismissed by the congressman and his staff. Intense anger quickly took over. In my initial e-mail to the congressman, I let him know what agencies I had or would be contacting on Sophie's behalf. They basically sent me back my own list. It was more than obvious to me that our congressman and his staff could care less about an elderly homeless lady and the nice couple who took her into their home. That e-mail left a sour spot in my stomach for that congressman. I still feel saddened by his response. I always had a whitewashed, dreamy vision of what politics could be in this country. Lately, the reality that our political system is more like a venomous cesspool and always has been was depressing to me. The passion for all things politics that I had since I was a child was becoming more of a source of frustration.

I grew up in Northeast Philadelphia, the Somerton section. Back in the day, my parents had a voting machine in our dining room every election day. Folks from the precinct came to our house on Delray Street to place their votes. I would sit on the sofa and watch them intently. I listened to every word of those voters' conversations, debates, and arguments as they waited in line for their turn to vote. I took in the way they were dressed. Some were all decked out in red, white, and blue and others in their Sunday best. I admired the passion of some, and I snickered at the stupidity of others. Of course, my most favorite part of election day and one of the reasons I loved having all those people come to our house to vote was the donuts. I loved the donuts. Everyone brought them to our house on election day.

I got in some trouble on the schoolyard at Saint Christopher's Catholic School.

I told the kids how Humphrey thought he was talking to a bunch of college students and spoke freely about how he thought young people were using their opposition to the war as escapism and ignoring domestic issues such as the Head Start Program, which he saved in a close senate vote. He was completely unaware there were several reporters in the room. I told the kids he lost to Nixon because of that. The nuns demanded to know where I heard such nonsense and told me to stop. Those nuns increased my hunger for all things political and created a love in me for our right to free speech. I do not think that was their intention.

I thought that our congressman was behaving the same way those young people acted back then. He seemed only interested in his own opposition to the way the wars in Iraq and Afghanistan were going. There was nothing wrong with his objections to how those wars were going. I'm quite sure we all had issues with the war. The problem was, he was only showing interest in and working on his war opposition and showing no interest in domestic problems in his own neighborhoods. He was a career military man that was now trying to be a career politician. He was missing the experience of being a neighbor in a civilian community. I was sure that it would eventually hurt his political career, and it did. He served only one term and then lost a senate bid.

The elderly woman that I was working with at that time had a beautiful home, three wonderful sons, and the most amazing grandchildren. From the outside looking in, it would appear she had everything you could ask for in life, except for happiness. The woman was so miserable. It took me weeks to get her to engage in some semblance of conversation. Once she did start talking, I became engrossed in the stories she told me of her childhood in Philadelphia and the discrimination her Italian family endured. They lived across the street from a Catholic school. The priest told her father his children had to go to a school in another parish a few blocks away because this school was for Irish kids. She continued to tell me her father, an expert carpenter, went on to do whatever he could for that Irish/Catholic school and church. He made shelves, desks, and did yard work. Eventually, the priest broke down and let the woman and her two brothers into the school. What a lesson that man taught his children. He killed them with kindness. Many small towns in and around the Philadelphia area and I suppose most American cities still have two parishes today. Of course, the domestic Catholic politics have changed. A lot of those second churches are barely holding on financially now, and many are being forced to close their doors.

That woman held a grudge against her father throughout her entire life because he would not let her go to college. Her one brother went to medical school, the other brother went to law school, and she got married and had three children. Now all these years later, here she was, sitting on a sofa in the den of her beautiful home, watching game show after game show, every Phillies baseball game, and occasionally, the news. She did not want the drapes opened as she preferred to sit in the dark. She had her meals and slept on that sofa. She had a gorgeous, screened back porch but refused to go out there. She could have gone anywhere. She could have taken cruises to warm and sunny islands. She could have gone to nice restaurants for lunches with family and friends. She could have hosted wonderful parties in her home. She chose to sit in the dark, eat chocolate pudding, and drink ginger ale.

I wanted to shout at her: *Do you have any idea how good your life could be? Do you know there are homeless people who have no one?*

Instead, I looked at her, really looked, and saw a sad, lonely woman who did not accomplish what she wanted to accomplish in her life. She was bitter and angry with her husband for dying suddenly ten years prior and leaving her alone. They had been saving all of their lives for retirement and had so many plans. She was sad she never had a daughter, and the list went on and on and seemed to have no end. She was proud of her sons and was happy to tell me and anyone else who would listen about all of their accomplishments, but she never told them. My heart was sad for her and her sons. I held her close to me and hugged her and told her she did the best she could with what she had. I told her it was never too late to change. She pulled away and did not believe me.

It hit me like lightening one afternoon as I sat listening to the third episode of a *Family Feud* marathon exactly what she was planning. She was rushing her death. More than anything, she did not want to be a further burden to her children or grandchildren. It was hard for me to accept, but if she wanted to sit in the dark and wither away, I would sit with her and be quiet. She earned the right to do what she wanted to do at this point in her life. Who are any of us to judge our elderly and the choices they make for their last days? Richard Dawson made her smile and occasionally, chuckle. That was close enough to her being happy for me.

She did eventually become fascinated by my stories about Sophie. She started to look forward to me coming to her house and sharing the latest Sophie news with her. It was such a relief to me to have her participating in a conversation every now and again. I started looking forward to my time with her too. She got to a point where she was asking questions and offering suggestions. What an amazing feeling to be able to connect with her. Now if I could just convince her family that it was okay for them to allow her to sit in the dark, eating only chocolate pudding, drinking ginger ale, and watching game shows all day and night, I would feel like I accomplished something huge.

I called Mr. White at the welfare office, public assistance office, or whatever we were supposed to call it these days again and left him another message. I wondered if I should write a letter to him, make a copy for myself, and then send it to him by certified mail.

Sister Marie from Catholic Social Services stopped by the house. She asked Sophie a ton of questions. I could tell Sophie was being evasive with her, and I wondered why. She asked Sophie about her mental health, something I had been afraid to do. Sophie beat around the bush and never gave a straight answer. She asked Sophie if she was supposed to be taking medication. There was something about the way Sophie answered no to that question that led me to believe she was supposed to be on medication. It was obvious Sophie had mental health issues, but I could not quite figure out what they were yet.

Sister Marie promised to go back to her office and figure out what she could do to help Sophie. She said she would get back to me some time during the next week. I was a bit agitated with Sophie for not being more forthcoming. I was also upset with Sister Marie for not taking Sophie with her. What exactly did Catholic Social Services do anyway?

Catholic Social Services is just another referral service, I thought. They refer you to an agency that is supposed to help find housing, but that agency sends you to another place to see if you qualify for the housing assistance. That agency needs paperwork you do not have, so they direct you to yet another agency. You could literally spend weeks jumping through all of these hoops and end up right where you started, which is nowhere and still homeless.

The mission statement of Catholic Social Services is to transform lives and bring about a just and compassionate society where *every* individual is valued, families are healthy and strong, and communities are united in their commitment to the good of all.

The organization has roots that date back to colonial Philadelphia. They offer family preservation services, foster care, adoption, immigration services, counseling, homeless services, senior citizen centers, care for the medically fragile, and adjudicated youth.

Why couldn't Sophie go to one of those senior citizen centers?

Many years ago when I became a foster mother for a little girl, I went to Catholic Social Services at Saint Michael's Church in Levittown, Pennsylvania, for counseling with the little girl's mother, so I know that they actually do counseling in-house. I also know that my church, Our Lady of Charity, provides meals and a few hours of shelter for the homeless in the basement of our church once a month.

These services are absolutely needed in communities all over the world, but I cannot help questioning what the responsibility of churches, civic organizations, and the individual family is in finding permanent, lasting solutions to the problems plaguing our cities and towns.

When the nun left, I asked Sophie why she did not answer her questions.

"I don't like her and I don't like God," she said.

I had no idea what to say to that, so I said nothing.

It dawned on me that Sophie had not been out of our house in more than a week. I asked her if there was somewhere I could take her or if she needed to take care of anything, and she said no, she just wanted to stay in the house. Was she afraid I would leave her somewhere? I won't lie to you the thought of leaving her somewhere did cross my mind more than once. I would never do it, but I did think about leaving her at all sorts of places.

Just imagining taking her out in public and the nightmare it could turn into was too much, but I knew she had to get out of the house for a while. I made a mental note to talk her into going out for a bit on my next day off from work.

I wondered if I should bother contacting other local politicians and agencies. The rejection I was getting was starting to sting a bit, so I decided to send only a few more e-mails.

Not one of those e-mails I sent received a reply. Sister Marie never returned either. When I finally reached her by phone, she told me there was nothing she or Catholic Social Services could do for Sophie. They tried to help Sophie previously, and she did not follow through. That explained Sophie's indifference during the interview. What a big disappointment.

I confronted Sophie. "Why would you not take the help they were giving you?" I asked.

Sophie's face changed. I could feel she was somewhere between angry and hurt. Hurt won out, and she started to cry.

"They tried to put me in a home with people that were really old. They were all in wheelchairs, or they walked with canes. They were all out of their minds. It was in a bad neighborhood too. I'm not like that. I still want to be young."

"Did you tell them how you felt?" I asked.

"They didn't listen to me."

There are politicians in this country that have common sense, and they are buying into the belief that the first thing homeless people need is a home. They understand that any other service is a waste of valuable money that could be used for housing.

San Jose, California, was home to a large homeless camp named the Jungle. The camp was home to men, women, and children. Many Fortune 500 companies are located within twenty miles of the Jungle. The city of San Jose led a massive effort not only to find housing for the homeless living in this camp but also to find employment for them.

The city government had no choice but to get involved because the Jungle was highly visible to those Fortune 500 employees as they sipped their lattes on their daily commute. The employees were not enjoying the scenery. They are probably good, charitable, and hardworking people. But with all the stress that comes with jobs and families, who could blame them for not wanting to see a homeless reality show on a daily basis?

When the bottom of our national economy fell out, California was hit hard. People were laid off from good-paying jobs and were unable to find comparable salaries; therefore, they could not afford the high cost of housing in the area.

Managing the homeless by criminalizing them or forcing them into our judicial systems, shelters, and temporary housing does not work. Putting the homeless in endless job training programs that never lead to permanent employment doesn't work either. The new focus has to be on permanent housing and employment.

Without an address, you cannot even apply for social services or any kind of government assistance. You cannot receive mail, send your children to school, or apply for a job. It's hard to think of these things when you are worried about where you are going to sleep, what you are going to eat, and how you are going to wash yourself and your clothes.

The leaders of two hundred communities across the country are buying into the concept that housing first makes perfect economical sense. In fact, the cost of transportation to and being seen in an emergency room along with a twenty-four-hour stay in a hospital is in many cases more than several months' rent on an apartment. It makes more sense to spend the money on the solution to the problem. It also makes sense to spend money on finding employment so these people can keep their homes.

Once safely in permanent housing and employed, these people become less of a burden on our public safety nets. They suddenly become taxpayers, giving back to the system that gave them a hand. Their children can once again thrive in school.

Deeper investments and financial and time commitments from public and private organizations, as well as information sharing between organizations and communities, and the Housing First model can stop the homeless epidemic in its tracks.

After calling Sister Marie again and asking her to clarify what happened between Catholic Social Services and Sophie, she told me Sophie did not like the nursing home and just walked out. They went on to place her in a group home, and Sophie just up and left there too. She also told me that John and I put ourselves in a difficult situation because her agency was now unable to list Sophie as homeless. Technically, she was living in a home, *our* home. That news came as a shock. Hopefully, there were other agencies that did not feel that way. I felt bad for Sister Marie. She was honestly trying to help us and Sophie, but her hands were tied. She could not force Sophie to accept the only help she could give her.

The situation, or should I say, the lack of direction and leadership from our politicians, county organizations, and religious institutions, frustrated me, to say the least. I took the rejection and lack of assistance so personally. They honestly made me feel less than like I didn't deserve help getting out of this situation with Sophie because John and I made a reckless decision when we took her in. I felt stupid, and at the same time, I was so angry with everyone. At least John and I did something. We did something that was real and hard. The right thing to do is never the easiest. An eighty-year-old woman was off of the streets, out of the woods, and safe and warm, and it still felt like it was the only thing we could do.

4

Thanks for Nothing

By the beginning of November, we had transformed Kathleen's bedroom into Sophie's bedroom. John's sister gave us a twin bed, a nightstand, and a dresser. She also gave us a recliner for our living room. It was light blue. That thrilled me, not that it was powder blue. That color blue did not go too well with the big bright-red sofa. I was happy because I wanted that big red sofa back.

I just kept saying to myself, "No worries, she will only be with us until we can find a good home for her." I still believed and was convinced one of her relatives would show up and claim her. They would knock on our front door and tell us they had been searching for her all over the county and could not thank us enough for keeping her safe and warm for them.

I would then feel all warm and fuzzy. I would feel like I did a good deed, and those feelings of doing the right thing would be validated. John and I would then be able to get back to building a life together—alone.

Mr. White *finally* answered his phone and informed me, proudly I might add, that Sophie had been on a waiting list for housing, but now that she was no longer *technically* homeless, her name had to be removed from the emergency housing list.

"She is still homeless," I pleaded with him.

His answer was that once we took her into our home, she was technically no longer considered homeless. That was what Catholic Social Services said too. Can you believe that? I was furious. No wonder we have such a homeless problem in this country. Why would anybody ever do *anything* to help when the organizations that are designed to help do nothing? He went on to tell me that he would be able to offer and set her up with some food stamps. However, before he could do that, I would have to make copies of all of Sophie's identification, type and certify a letter saying she resided at our address, register her at the post office, and fill out a "landlord" statement that he was going to send to me, and I needed to have that certified as well.

I realized that by doing everything he asked me to do, it would mean that we would basically be stuck with Sophie indefinitely. She would be our tenant. There are laws in Pennsylvania protecting tenants from eviction. We were only trying to help her out, to keep her out of the cold, and now if we wanted her to leave our home, we would have to take her to court. I understood completely why that law was so important, but wow, in this situation, it really seemed so wrong. I decided to take my chances anyway and believe that because I only had good intentions, all would turn out well. I wanted to get as much help set up for her as possible, so when we did eventually find a home for her, she would be able to keep that roof over her head.

It took a few frustrating weeks, but I managed to do everything Mr. White requested of me. Sophie was so untrusting of my intentions. Over and over again, I explained to her that there was nothing the Chester Office of Assistance had that I wanted. I reassured her I was just trying to help her. Finally, she produced her identification for me. I took her upstairs into my office to make copies. I had her watch as I put the copies in the envelope sealed and addressed it to Mr. White. I gave her the originals back and watched her put them into that ratty-looking pocketbook of hers.

About four weeks later, I received a letter from Mr. White. Sophie was eligible to receive fifteen dollars a month in food stamps. I kid you not. I spent more than that on postage and the notary, not to mention the time it took to get all of the paperwork together. There was no word on the housing assistance, and he had no idea when we would have any news on a suitable home for her.

In the meantime, Sophie told me she had two storage units and needed to go make payments on them. She also told me she had to go to the bank. It was the first time I heard of any bank account, so I could not wait to see where the day would lead.

Sophie was dressed in a cute outfit. It was one I had given her. I was a bit surprised she took my suggestion and decided to wear the green slacks and matching green sweater. She refused to use the pocketbook I gave her and insisted on carrying her own old and tattered bag with the broken strap. I was curious to know what was in that bag and scared to know at the same time. Regardless, she looked so much better than she did that first night when John brought her into our home. I gave her my cherished *Bucks County Courier Times* newspaper burgundy jacket because she only had a thin sweater. She liked the jacket and was so happy it had deep pockets that zippered so people couldn't steal her stuff and she would not lose anything.

When I opened the front door and announced let's go, the color drained from Sophie's face. She said her arm and leg hurt, and she wanted to go another day.

Inside, I was deeply annoyed, but I smiled and said, "Sophie, I want to hurry and get this done so we can get home and watch our soaps. You don't want to lose your stuff that is in the storage, do you?"

She developed a limp and a whine and made her way to the car. I helped her put on her seatbelt. I could still see immense fear in her face, so I continued to talk about things we could do once we returned home. I wanted to reassure her she was going home with me.

Once we got onto MacDade Boulevard, Sophie was able to direct me to her bank, which was located in the town of Glenolden. We went into the Wells Fargo bank and sat down. It was busy. Sophie explained to me that there was only one person in the bank that could help her, and that woman had customers in her cubby. When it was Sophie's turn, I stayed in the lobby and Sophie went into the office. When she was done with her banking business, Sophie asked me to come into the office, and she introduced me to Marie. Marie told me Sophie received a social security check and a small pension every month. The funds were directly deposited into her account on the third day of the month. The woman was very kind and patient with Sophie. It was nice to see considering the rest of the bank employees seemed to glare disapprovingly of Sophie and me. I felt angry with myself because I let them make me feel embarrassed. I let a bunch of selfish, ignorant people with no clue cause me to feel embarrassed. That was so frustrating. I told Marie that John and I were going to do our best to help Sophie get back on her feet and keep her safe.

I was not familiar with driving in the Upper Darby area at that time. I knew my father lived there as a kid, and I knew of Michael Chitwood, the very popular and colorful yet effective police superintendent, because his son was the police chief in Daytona Beach where my parents live now. Demographically, I had no clue, so it was no wonder we were hopelessly lost, trying to find one of the storage facilities.

To keep from totally stressing out, I asked Sophie what was in the storage facility. She told me she collected Elvis memorabilia ever since she was a teenager. She said she had a lot of it in storage until something bad happened. She said there was an Elvis impersonator named Jim "E" Curtin. Sophie said she loved to go see him perform and that she always took pictures for him. She told me they were friends until he got a girlfriend. Sophie told the girlfriend about her Elvis collection. The girlfriend wanted to see it, so Soph brought her to the storage place. The woman beat Sophie up, stole her memorabilia, and left her lying injured in the storage unit. The person working at the facility called the police, and they took Sophie to the hospital. The hospital treated her injuries and then put her in the psych ward for twenty-four hours. Sophie said they did not believe her.

I do not know how I managed to hold it together at that point. I was boiling mad. I did see adds for this Elvis impersonator in our local newspaper. He definitely did exist and perform in our area. I believed her story. I could tell how hurt she was as she told me what happened. Did this Jim person betray her? Did he even know what his girlfriend did to Sophie? I knew I wanted to go see him perform and to ask him a few questions.

We finally found the place, which honestly was hard to miss. That was the kind of day we were having. Sophie said she would go in by herself. I sat in the car and turned up the radio. After only a few minutes, Sophie returned visibly upset. The woman, she told me, would not accept her payment and was going to sell all of her stuff. My dream of a quick and easy time of running these errands completely evaporated. I sat there in the car for a minute, stunned. I shut off the radio and the car and went into that office.

I asked the woman who had a visible attitude what the problem was. She told me she could not take any payment unless it was a full payment.

I thought, *What do you think you are, a mortgage company?*

She told me Sophie was chronically late with her payments and owed late fees. I asked if she eventually made her payments in full.

The woman answered, "Yes, always."

I asked how much Sophie was behind, expecting to hear hundreds of dollars, and the woman said fifteen dollars. The fifteen dollars was merely a late payment fee. Again, I was stunned for a moment or two. I asked if she new Sophie's situation, if she knew she had no transportation, and if she was aware the poor woman did not even have a roof over her head.

She said yes. She was aware of Sophie's dilemma, but they could not make any exceptions.

I wondered what I would have done if the roles were reversed, and this was my job. I wanted to think I knew what I would do. I would call the police and ask them what I should do to help this poor homeless woman. I would have made an exception and told my boss to stuff his rules in this situation. I would take the fifteen dollars out of my wallet and pay it for her if this was my job. I did just that and gave the woman the lousy fifteen dollars and asked for a receipt for myself and one for Sophie. I asked when the next payment was due and told her I would mail it to her. I asked for a business card so I would have the phone number and the address. She apologized and smiled a fake smile. I could tell she wanted to be sarcastic, but I did ask for the phone number, and she probably sensed I was going to call the owner. She was suddenly afraid I was going to call her boss, and she was exactly right. That was my intention. I could not even smile back. I imagined this was the same piece of scum that was here that day that Sophie was beaten up in her storage unit. She probably did not lift one finger to help her.

I asked Sophie if she wanted to go look at her stuff, maybe get a few of her own things for her room. She quickly said no. I hoped she was not afraid of me. Was she feeling that I would hurt her or take any of her stuff?

She was gloating by the time we drove away. It made me feel good to see her smile. It felt good to stand up for someone. That was something I often had trouble doing for myself.

We found the next facility a bit easier, and Sophie made her payment. The man at the storage place in Glenolden was nice. He asked Sophie how she was doing and introduced himself to me.

It dawned on me after she made *that* payment that she had more money on her, so she had just refused to pay the extra fifteen-dollar late fee at the other facility. I shook it off.

She asked if we could stop by to visit a friend of hers who had a business on MacDade Boulevard. I was nervous about what kind of person this friend might be but also hopeful that I may possibly learn something more about Sophie and how she came to be homeless.

We went into the office, and Sophie introduced me to Lisa. We were both cautious of one another. I was trying to figure out what kind of business this was. There were two desks and lots of paperwork and files piled up throughout the office. Lisa was tall with dark hair, and I couldn't help but notice her sad eyes. I sensed this woman had a story to tell. I liked her immediately and sensed she only had Sophie's best interest at heart. She handed Sophie some mail. I told her we would stop back the following week, and I asked Lisa not to tell anyone where Sophie was staying. A few women in the area were cruel to Sophie, and a few others robbed her. Lisa's business was just a few doors down from the twelve-step meeting place were Sophie used to stay. She agreed it was a good idea if no one knew where Sophie was staying, for now.

We stopped at McDonald's before heading home. I felt bad feeding her at McDonald's considering that was what she ate for months when she was wandering the streets. Sophie insisted she loved the cheeseburgers. I was just hungry. She took her double cheeseburger apart and wrapped half of it back up. She said she would save that part for later.

That is pitiful, I thought.

I looked forward to cooking a nice warm meal for her that night.

As the two of us headed back down MacDade Boulevard, Sophie pointed to a building and said it was her doctor's office. I tried to get the name from the sign but drove by too fast. I made a mental note of the surroundings so I could get the doctor's name on another trip.

She also pointed out the patch of woods where she would go to spend the night. I looked around at the people walking their dogs or chasing their children, and I tried to picture Sophie walking by them with her shopping cart full of plastic bags. Did they notice her? How could I blame them when I never used to notice her or the others? We are so uncomfortable with mental illness. We are terrified of what we do not understand. I understand a little bit about mental illness, and I am still terrified.

Out of the blue, John called and asked if I wanted two little dogs. What in this world was this man thinking? Faith, his big all-white German shepherd, passed away last March. I loved him. He was such a good dog. He was also a lot of work. Shiny white hair was all over the house, all the time. He needed to be brushed, bathed, fed, and so much more. I did not want one dog, let alone two.

That night, he explained to me that the dogs belonged to his ex-wife and her daughter. My stepson Michael asked if we could take the dogs because his mom was moving to a new and into an apartment and could not have them there. I still not want them. I wanted a cat. Cats are just there. Every once in a while, usually just when you need them the most, they appear to give you a little love. They are quiet. They do not have to go out. They do not require sitters. The only downside to a cat for me would be breathing. I am allergic.

John printed the pictures of the dogs from his e-mail. Once I looked at the pictures, it was all over. They were so cute.

I was a bit shocked that John would even entertain the idea of little dogs. Once I got used to the idea that I was going to be a doggie parent again, I looked forward to their arrival. I was stressed about the fact the little guys would be flying alone from Denver to Philadelphia. The vet would be giving them medication that would keep them calm and hopefully asleep for the duration of the flight. Would they like us?

Sophie was not even a little bit happy about the impending arrival of the dogs.

"Me no like dogs," she whined.

I tried to convince her, as well as myself, that they would be good company for her while John and I were at work. Michael put in a doggie door for us. It was actually a glass insert with the doggy door in the bottom that fit on the track of our sliding door. It pretty much eliminated our use of that door. We could now only open the slider halfway. It would have to work because I did not want Sophie to be responsible for letting the dogs in and out of the house.

I had fun picking out their little bowls, a basket for their toys, and of course, plenty of toys. They were three and four years old, so I was sure they still played.

A few days later, our boys were on their way. As luck would have it, so was our first winter storm. I watched as flight tracker listed one delay after another. They sat on the runway in Denver

hours. I was frantic. The medication would
. They were probably so scared. I tried to stay
while John and Michael went to the airport.
house making sure there was nothing they
get into that would harm them.

I was so .... d when John finally called two hours later
to tell me they were on the ground. He called again to tell me
they would be a while because both dogs were vomiting. They
wanted them to calm down a bit before putting them back in
the crates and into the car.

The rain finally stopped just as they arrived home. As soon
as Lance and Louie walked through the door, I was in love with
them. I couldn't even get mad when Louie walked right over
to John's Harley–Davidson boots and peed on them. Sophie
even laughed about that one. It was Louie's world from that
minute on.

John, Michael, and I took turns taking them out into the
yard and showing them how to use the doggie door. We hadn't
laughed that much in a long time. The yard was fenced, but we
wanted to make sure there was nothing we were missing out
there that could hurt them. They looked exhausted, so we took
their beds up into our room. They walked around the room,
investigating and smelling everything. I made sure I put all of
our shoes in the closet and shut the door. Louie tried hopping
into bed with us a couple of times during the night. I got up
and put him back in his bed. I had a little dog, Chelsea, and
she would sleep on top of me. It was awful, so I didn't want
to start that habit with these guys. They finally fell asleep and
slept through the night. John and I were like worried brand-
new parents, and we were up all night checking on them.

My thoughts were all over the place that night. How in the
world did we go from an empty nest to having an elderly woman
and two yappy little dogs under our roof in a matter of weeks? I

wondered what people were going to think of us taking Sophie into our home. Would they think it was a kind thing to do, or would they think we were crazy?

I wondered how people like Mr. White could stand doing the job they did. I wondered if they realized they were not actually helping people. Maybe they were so out of touch and didn't even realize how ridiculous fifteen dollars a month in food stamps sounded. Most likely, there wasn't anything they could do about it. It was their job, and they had to do what they had to do.

Public assistance was only the beginning. Somehow, I knew figuring out and dealing with Medicare and Medicaid were going to be another nightmare. Those hoops would have to wait.

Years earlier, when I worked as a Pizza Hut manager, I slipped on some oil and injured my back and tore the cartilage in my knee. I needed to be out of work to recover after several surgeries. There was a lapse in the time of my last paycheck and when my disability pay started. Mistakes were made, and it was quite a while before I received any payments at all and even longer before the amount was correct. In the meantime, I was a single mom and nearly exhausted the small amount of savings I had. A friend suggested I apply for public assistance. I was honestly scared to apply. Back then, you had to show up at a payment center every other week. There were dozens of people, pushy people in the line, and there were also all sorts of line jumpers. The process could take a couple of hours. Besides being a frightening experience, it was also mortifying to me. It made me angry because I never should have been there. I paid into my disability fund for years. It was my own money that was being kept from me. Honestly, I felt like I was better than that, better than the other people in that line were. Of course, I quickly realized I wasn't any better than most of the women there. There were other women like me. Some were dealing with health issues and waiting for insurance payments. We quickly realized how grateful we should feel that we had this safety net. There was a young woman who was in the foster care system her whole life. She became pregnant at eighteen and got kicked out of her house, and now she was trying to be a good mom and go to school. I met women on that line that had been brutally abused and finally had the strength to get away. Several times, we had to surround her because her ex knew she would be there to pick up her benefits and he would show up and try to get to her. It was terrifying and at the same time empowering. The whole experience was humbling for sure. As much as I hated that line, it was an education for me. Everyone I met there had a story to tell, and I became fascinated with all of them, and empathy and compassion chased away my ignorance.

As enlightening as that experience was for me, I was thrilled when it was over and vowed I would always be prepared financially for emergencies. I never wanted to see that line again. It is different now. Those on assistance receive debit cards. No more lines. I think that is such a good thing. Looking back, I wouldn't want to change my experience, but I am glad people are no longer subjected to that insanity. At the same time, without the stigma, I wonder what inspires people to become self-sufficient. When something makes us uncomfortable, we instinctively do whatever we can to be more comfortable.

My daughter invited the entire family and included Sophie for Thanksgiving dinner that year. Sophie was excited about going until the last minute. All of a sudden, she was refusing to go with us. We had no choice but to leave her home alone with the dogs. The whole time we were at my daughter's house, I wondered what was happening at our house. That wondering turned to worry about Sophie and the dogs. It was hard to enjoy ourselves, so we left early. My daughter prepared a nice plate for Sophie. She was thrilled when we gave it to her. It appeared she hadn't moved out of the chair the entire time we were gone. She had Louie on her lap. I was so happy to see the two of them bonding. That happy feeling lasted a few minutes before I asked John if he felt like she would ever be mean to Lance. He laughed at me. Lance just wasn't a fan of cuddling the way Louie was. Lance was more interested in chasing squirrels and eating.

I did some research and was able to find out that the Elvis impersonator Sophie was friends with, Jim "E" Curtin, claimed to have seen Elvis perform fifty-one times. He also claimed to have been given a jumpsuit personally by Elvis, as well as numerous other souvenirs. Over the years, he supposedly amassed a collection of more than fifty thousand pieces of Elvis memorabilia. He was in a relationship with a woman named Renata for more than twelve years. Frustrated that he never married her, she left him. After she left, he then lost five loved ones in one year—his mom, dad, a brother, an uncle, and the president of his fan club. He tried unsuccessfully for three years to win Renata back. When his attempts to get her back failed, he became depressed and began to sell off his memorabilia collection.

I needed to do some more research to find out who this new girlfriend of his was. Sophie said the woman was trying to impress and keep Jim by giving him the Elvis memorabilia items that she was stealing from Sophie and others. I had a feeling there was so much more to this story.

I could hardly wait to take Sophie to the grocery store to use her brand-new Access debit card. Not really. I was dreading that expedition.

5

Little Feet and Big Broken Hearts

My granddaughters Morgan and Avery were coming to spend the weekend with us. They were only three and six years old. I was worried about how they would react to Sophie. I was also worried about how Sophie would react to them. I shuddered when the thought of her harming them popped into my head. I felt I knew enough of her personality at this point to doubt she would harm a child. I would be diligent anyway and not let my guard down.

I asked her if she had any grandchildren, and she told me again that her son Frankie had a cute little girl. The little girl's mother was the one Soph said had plastic surgery so Frankie would think she was younger and get back together with her. She would not tell me the woman's name or the little girl's name. She told me her and Frankie were planning to get an apartment together when the woman tricked him into moving to California with her. Sophie said Frankie left her sitting on a sidewalk, crying with no place to go.

I think Frankie's girlfriend deserves a man like Frankie and vise versa. If he left his own mother on the sidewalk, homeless, did she think for one minute he would never leave her? My grandmother once told me that if you want to know how a man will treat you, just listen to how he talks to or about and watch how he treats his own mother and/or his sisters. Examine those relationships, and chances are that is exactly how he will treat you. I am so grateful John loved and respected his mother, and he adores his six older sisters.

I was hoping she would tell me something about her daughter and her daughter's children or the son that lived in the area and his children, if he had any.

I had to remind myself I was only hearing Sophie's side of the story. I was not a fan of my own mother. But I would never leave the woman homeless. Most likely, I would pay someone to take care of her. I had my reasons for disliking her immensely. It was possible Sophie's kids had legitimate reasons for abandoning her. I wondered if I would ever know the other sides of Sophie's story.

Another concern with the kids coming to visit was the dogs. They were not used to being around small children, so we had no idea how they would react. I was nervous. I read a couple of blog posts on how to introduce dogs to children. There was a lot to learn. We decided to have the dogs on their leashes so we could control them when the kids first came into the house. We also gave the kids special homemade peanut butter treats to feed the dogs. Those treats would be reserved for only the kids to give to them.

I worried for nothing. It was love at first sight for the dogs and the kids. Lance and Louie followed the little girls around like lovesick little puppies. They continue to do that today. All we have to do is say the kids are coming over, and they head for the front window to sit and wait, tails wagging.

Morgan and Avery took to Sophie immediately. Their mother, my youngest daughter, worked at a Sunrise Senior Living facility, so the girls were used to being around elderly people. Sophie smiled a lot while the girls were with us. It was nice to see this side of her. It was nice to see her happy.

Three-year-old Avery was potty training, and Sophie said she had the tiniest hiney she ever saw. She started to call Avery "tiny hiney." We thought it was cute, but Avery did not like the nickname one bit.

She would scrunch up her little face and tell Sophie, "That is *not* my name. I am Avery Paige."

We would all laugh, and Avery would stomp away. She still doesn't like it at all.

Sophie was getting used to having the television in our living room completely to herself. She watched the soap channel 24-7. I was noticing more and more that she was not even going to into her room to sleep at night. She had been sleeping in the blue recliner in her clothes. I needed to figure out a way to put a stop to that. I decided we needed a TV for her room. John's sister came to our rescue. She gave us a TV for Sophie's room. It was larger and nicer than the one we had in the living room, but she refused to watch it in her room.

In the meantime, she seemed to get agitated around the fifth episode of *Dora the Explorer*, so I took the girls upstairs into our bedroom to watch their shows. It annoyed me, but it seemed easier to bring the girls upstairs. Everybody would be happy that way, except for me.

By Sunday afternoon, it dawned on me that I had not stopped the entire weekend. I cooked, served, cleaned, shopped, bathed the little ones, the dogs, and started Sophie's baths and did all of our laundry. I was exhausted. Not that I was one bit unhappy, I was just plain tired. All in all, the weekend went well. The dogs didn't bite the kids, and the kids didn't bite the dogs. Sophie couldn't bite anybody because she didn't have any teeth. She was nice to the girls and the dogs, and they were nice to her.

I planned to talk to Sophie about contributing more to the household chores and doing more for herself, especially when the little ones were visiting. If she was going to be staying here for at least the immediate future, I was going to stop treating her like a guest. My time with the kids was so limited that I wanted to be with them, and not cleaning. Sophie was just going to have to understand that. I was starting to feel a bit resentful. I felt like she was taking advantage of me. I decided to run the idea by John. I wanted to know if he had any suggestions on how to approach the subject with Sophie so I wouldn't sound rude or mean.

When our grandsons met Sophie, they thought she was hysterical. They liked the way she talked without her teeth. They were very curious about where she came from. We did not tell any of the younger kids that she was homeless. We just told them that she was a friend and she needed a place to stay for a little while. The older girls, Allyson and Julia, being teenagers were a bit more curious. We told them the truth. They were always just a bit more skeptical of Sophie, and Sophie was unsure of them. Sophie knew they did not trust her. She gave them dirty looks, so of course they reciprocated. It was funny to watch, but at the same time, it was sad. Sophie exhibited so many childlike behaviors. She would stick her tongue out at Allyson and mumble mean things to her when she thought I wasn't listening. I wondered if her issues stemmed from a form of disability, as well as some sort of mental illness.

I could feel how much she missed her own grandchildren. I can't explain why I felt that I just did. Why didn't they miss her? My heart would break if I didn't know where my grandkids were. It would be amazing if we could facilitate a reunion with her family for her.

John thought it would be fair to ask her to load the dishwasher, run it, and put the dishes away. We decided she should also clean her own room and bathroom. I am oddly obsessed with having my dishwasher loaded a certain way. John thought it would be a good idea to show her how I wanted it done. When she agreed so easily to the chores, I decided to suck it up and let her do it however she wanted. If she didn't get it done the exact way I liked it, I would have to learn to be okay with that.

When I got home from work the next day, the dishwasher had not been run. It looked like she opened the door and just laid everything in there with no order or direction. Cups were on their sides, plates were strewn about on top of the spines, and the silverware wasn't in the silverware bins—it was scattered throughout the upper basket. It was unbelievable and quickly becoming nearly impossible for me to remain patient. Had she seriously never loaded a dishwasher before? I took everything out, rinsed all the dishes, and reloaded the dishwasher. I made myself a cup of tea and tried to calm myself down. I walked into the living room and put a cup of tea on the end table next to her. Taking a deep breath, I looked at her and asked her why she put the dishes in the dishwasher the way she did.

"Me forgot what you said," she answered while looking at the floor. There was no doubt in my mind that this woman was going to drive me crazy.

Another shock that day was realizing that she was taking out and eating ice-cold all of the nice lunches I was leaving in the refrigerator for her. I found out because I left my tea in the microwave that morning. It was still in there when I got home. It was obvious she could not use the microwave. I could not believe she never said anything. How was it even possible that she never used a microwave? I asked her to come in the kitchen so I could show her how to use it again. I asked her to do it in front of me. She could not remember how to set the time. I tried setting the time so all she had to do was to push start. She could not even do that. I was so frustrated with her and what I assumed was a lack of effort on her part.

The feelings I was having at that time were so unfamiliar to me. It wasn't like me to be so impatient with someone who was so obviously mentally challenged. It was not like me to feel sorry for myself either, but here I was, standing in my kitchen, wondering what I had done to deserve to have to put up with this woman in my house. All I wanted was to have a nice life with my husband, our kids and grandkids, and our little dogs. I wanted her gone. I was not an angel or a saint, and I was tired of being called one. No angel or saint would ever feel the way I was feeling that day.

I wanted to put her and her ratty shopping bags and broken pocketbook into my car and drive her to that school on MacDade Boulevard and tell her to get out of my car and go back into those woods and stay there. Have fun getting water for your friends back there. In my mind, I imagined leaving her and all of her dirty stuff in those woods and driving away. The thought of driving away did not make me feel good at all. As much as I wished at that time it could make me feel good, I knew that wasn't the way I was made. Why did I have to care so much? Why did doing the right thing always have to be so hard and take so darned long?

I knew Sophie was not just mentally ill. She was also challenged in some other way. It was not Down's syndrome. Autistic. Maybe some other kind of syndrome, or it was possible she was just slow. Was stroke a possibility? She was eighty years old. There was no doubt I needed to take her to see her doctor. I wondered why every time I brought it up, she changed the subject or flat-out told me she did not need to go see him. She insisted she liked the guy and did not want to see any other doctor. John would have to talk to her. He would have to convince her that she needed to have a checkup.

Whatever her issues, diagnosis, or crisis, the fact was she needed compassion and real help from us. She did not need referral services. She needed a home, a safe place to live, and some help managing that home and her life. Perhaps she needed to be in some sort of facility. I decided to look into some assisted living homes instead of continuing to run around in circles for people that had no intention or resources to help Sophie find a home of her own.

I wondered how she ever managed to care for her children, herself, or a home. How could anyone think it was okay to leave this helpless person alone? Where were her sisters and brothers, nieces and nephews? What sin did this woman commit that caused her to be shunned by every one of her relatives, her own children, friends, and her entire community?

It got to the point where it was easier for me to do everything myself for the sake of getting things done. Sophie was perfectly content to sit in the blue recliner and watch me run around the house like a nut. For me, it made perfect sense at the time. I didn't realize I was enabling her helplessness and creating a life of servitude for myself.

The first week of December, John got a call from his sister Nancy in Florida. She told him their father was in the hospital with pneumonia. Something about the news this time didn't sit well with him. He was concerned. He could not shake the gut feeling that he needed to go see his father. After speaking with his sisters, he made the decision to leave for Florida the next night after work. Two of his sisters would make the drive with him. There was no time to make arrangements for Sophie, the dogs, and my job, so it was decided I would stay home. It was the first time John and I would be spending any time apart since we were married. I was worried about him driving through the night. We make the drive from Philadelphia to Florida several times a year, and he never wanted to stop and rest. I made him promise to let either one or both of his sisters take turns sharing the driving. I thought it was a bit bizarre that he packed his motorcycle into the trailer and decided to take it with them. We usually took the bike and trailer with us for the bike weeks in Daytona, but it was December. When I asked John about it, he said he thought it would be a good idea to have an extra vehicle with them because there would be three of them. I still thought it was odd.

We both got home from work the following night around nine fifteen. While John packed his suitcase, I put together some sandwiches, drinks, and snacks. I made a pot of coffee. His sisters Sue and Pat arrived a few minutes later. The three of them were on the road before ten o'clock. I felt so alone once they pulled away. I was worried about my husband and my father-in-law. John was still grieving the loss of his mother. He wasn't prepared emotionally to lose his father. Not even close. I tossed and turned the entire night.

Early the next morning, I opened my eyes to see Sophie standing over me, scowling and gritting her gums.

"Where is my money?" She was practically touching my face with her face. I was frozen by fear. "You stole my money." Her face was all screwed up, and she was spitting through her gritted gums.

My first instinct was to look for her hands to make sure she didn't have some kind of a weapon. I didn't see anything in her hands. I took a deep breath. She demanded again, three maybe four times, for me to give it back to her. The more awake I became, the more filled with anger I became.

I could barely see through the red swirling in my mind. What was this lunatic thinking? How dare she scare me this way! I knew I had to pull it together and get up. I needed to get away from her. She was so done. How could I have felt sorry for her? What the heck is wrong with me that I continuously allow these crazy, out-of-control people into my life? In one svelte ninja move, I slipped over to the other side of the bed and jumped up.

"I do not have any idea what you are talking about." I told her firmly. Feeling more in control now that I was out from under her, my sanity slowly returned. "If you let me wake up and pull myself together, I promise you I will come downstairs and help you find whatever it is you are missing."

She cursed and continued screaming at me, swearing and insisting that I took money from her. I told her to get out of my room. I practically pushed her out the door. I shut my door loudly and locked it, not caring if she heard it lock this time. I was boiling mad and wondered what would happen if I called the police. They would most likely take her to the emergency room and keep her for twenty-four to forty-eight hours and then let her go, not caring that it was frigid outside and she had nowhere to go. I went back and forth with caring and not caring if she froze to death. I was so scared and angry. I was mad at myself for not remembering to lock the darn door the night before. This is what I was afraid of since the first night she stayed with us. It was the first time since she arrived that I left the bedroom door unlocked. Had she tried to get in before? I started wondering what she was doing downstairs. Was she trying to hurt herself? Was she planning to leave? Oh my goodness, I wondered if she would hurt the dogs to get back at me. I unlocked the door, and Lance and Louie bounced into the bedroom. I slammed the door shut and locked it again. The dogs looked confused. I was relieved that they were safe with me. Why did this have to happen while John was gone? I misdirected my anger toward him. How dare he leave me here alone with her? I was so confused, and I could not wait until he called. If they drove throughout the night, they would be getting close to Florida. It was weird that she suddenly wasn't talking like a baby. My anger was being replaced with me feeling like a total idiot.

I could not stay locked up in my room forever. Feeling stronger, I took a shower and then went downstairs to make breakfast. I calmly asked Sophie what she was missing.

"One hundred and fifty dollars," she mumbled. "I'd give it to ya if you asked," she half whined to me while putting her head down.

"I know you would, Sophie, and I promise you, I did not take anything from you. Let's go in your room, and I will help you look for your money."

If she attacked me in any way, I knew I could hurt her. She was after all eighty years old. The problem was, I did not want to hurt her. I did not want to live with that memory. I said a few quick prayers to Saint Anthony, the patron saint of the lost. I asked him, while he was at it, to help us locate Sophie's lost family too.

Thirty-five minutes later, I found the crumpled bills underneath of her nightstand along with some sort of crumbs. I told her she scared me that morning and I would appreciate if she never came into my bedroom again. I told her again that I would never ever take anything from her. She appeared to feel remorseful.

I said it again. "Do not ever come into my bedroom again. Do you understand that?"

She put her head down and whispered, "Okay, me won't." The baby talk was back. I liked it much better than the mean talk she used earlier that morning.

I have a history with post traumatic stress disorder, or PTSD. It started when I was sexually assaulted as a child and escalated when my brother was murdered in a random road rage attack. I worked so hard for many years with a therapist to get past my irrational fears and panic attacks. I was still angry with Sophie for scaring me in my own home, but I was more upset with myself for allowing her to frighten me. I wasn't sure if I would be able to forgive her for that behavior. I missed John. I always felt safe with him.

When he called, I asked about his father first. He said his father was surprised to see him and more surprised to see his daughters. He was already feeling better, but John said he felt as if he should be there a bit longer, and they were all happy they made the decision to take the trip. They were having a good visit with their dad and with their sister Nancy and her family. Frank lived in Port Orange, Florida, with Nancy and her family. My parents also lived in Port Orange, just outside of Daytona Beach. It was another coincidence we discovered when we first met. John and I of course do not believe in coincidences, but we did think it was interesting, to say the least, that we each had a father with the same first name, the same middle name, and living in the same town in another state. And both of our fathers were artists.

I wondered if I should tell him at this point what Sophie had done. It would no doubt upset him. Maybe I should wait until he gets home. The last thing I wanted him to do was to worry about me. I decided to tell him anyway. He would have been upset with me if I didn't. When I told him what happened that morning, he was furious. He told me to put Sophie on the phone. He told her if she ever did anything like that again, she would have to leave and would never be welcome in our home again. He told her to apologize to me. She gave me such angry, dirty looks while she was listening to him. When she hung up, I told her that I tell John everything and I would never keep anything from him. She apologized to me again and continued to apologize for days. She did everything I asked her to do, including taking a bath. Later that night, she tried to give me the one hundred and fifty dollars. I told her I did not want her money. I asked her to keep it in her pocketbook. I made a mental to pick up a wallet for her.

A few days later, John's father took a turn for the worst, and he passed away. He seemed to be getting better, so it was a bit of a shock. We were all grateful that John and his sisters made that trip. Only eight months before, his mother passed away.

The month before we lost his mother, we lost Faith, John's pure-white German shepherd. Faith was thirteen years old and had been his constant companion since the loss of his seventeen-year-old son John to suicide.

I asked John why he named his male dog Faith. He said because he needed a lot of it at the time, and he figured that whenever he called the dog's name, it would remind him that he needed to have faith. The dog got him through his struggle for sobriety and then the grief of losing his oldest child. I fell in love with Faith the first time I met him. He was so sweet, unless you were a stranger with unkind intentions. I witnessed Faith's loyalty to his family when a man from a medical supply company was up to no good in my mother-in-law's bedroom. Faith lunged over furniture and several people to get to that guy, and he was lucky to have made it out the front door with all of his extremities. When I went into my mother-in-law's bedroom, her pocketbook was thrown on the floor and open.

Before that incident with the man from the medical supply company, Faith started having trouble making it up the stairs to sleep with us at night. We were able to find the right combination of medicines to give him some relief from his pain, and he had been feeling like a puppy again. In the middle of one night, Faith woke John by licking his face. That was very odd. Usually when he needed to go out during the night, he would bark at the bedroom door until one of us got up and let him out. Startled, we both sat up. Faith paced back and forth until John got out of bed and walked to the corner of the room where

Faith usually slept. When the dog lay down on his blanket, John lay down on the floor next to him, and my heart sank. I started to pray and closed my eyes tight, trying to stop the tears. A few minutes later, Faith was gone. As heartbroken as we were, we were both so grateful he didn't suffer and that we didn't have to make the decision no pet lover ever wants to make.

That year was a heartbreaking and life-changing year for our family. In our few short years of being together, John and I saw our share of sorrow. We also realized we had a lot of blessings to be grateful for and still had so much more life to look forward too.

6

Attention Walmart Shoppers

The funeral mass for John's father was held on December 17 at St. Andrew's Church in Drexel Hill, Pennsylvania. Frank McGettigan was a talented and well-respected architect, a friend to many, and a good father. All of his children respected and adored him.

Saint Andrew's is one of my favorite churches in our area. I remember Kathleen telling me that Frank designed the church's new roof and ceiling. The building is heavy with old stone and thick wood on both the interior and the exterior of the building. It reminds me of what I always imagined an old castle might look like. It first opened in June 1916.

A number of John's childhood friends attended the mass and the funeral. The circumstances were sad, but it was nice to meet them. It amazed me that he still stayed in contact with his oldest friends. I lived in several different areas as a child, so it was hard to keep up with my old and new friends.

It was brutally cold and windy that day. John's sisters scheduled a luncheon after the services at Anthony's in Drexel Hill. It was a lovely get-together, but for a sad reason. John held up well throughout the day. I knew he was hurting deeply but insisted on being strong for his sisters and brother.

Christmas that year was the chaotic whirlwind it always was, and just as quickly as it arrived, it was gone. We all did our best to cheer John up, but his heart was hurting. We spent most of the holiday week visiting our kids' homes. Because the grandchildren were so young, it was hard to get them to separate from home and their new toys. I was thrilled that John's son, Michael, joined us at my daughter's house for Christmas Eve. That was the first time I saw John smile in weeks. It warmed my heart, and I was grateful for all of our kids. It was so important to both John and I that our kids not only know one another but for them to be comfortable with and to like each other. It would be awful for our children to have to attend mine or John's funeral and for them to feel uncomfortable because they were complete strangers. Remarrying as the parent of adult children and grandchildren can be awkward and challenging, to say the least. It was a big relief to both John and I that our kids liked each other, and they were getting along so well.

We were all going to be happy to put the sadness of the past year behind us and anxious to see what the New Year had in store for us. We both knew from experience that grief is not something you can ever get over but more like something you have to get through. We also knew we would have to work hard to find our new normal.

Sophie was invited everywhere we were invited, but she refused to go anywhere that involved socializing with us. When I asked her why she didn't want to be around people, she said she was tired. She was starting to exhibit some depression symptoms. She was literally stuck here with us, and most likely, she was desperately missing her own family. Who wouldn't be missing their children and grandchildren especially during the holidays? John said Sophie was probably thrilled to be with us because it was more than obvious her own family was full of losers that could care less for her or her safety and well-being. I do not think you ever stop missing them even if they are not who you wished they were. I was sad for her and angry with her family whoever and wherever they were. Trying to cheer her up was good for both John and I.

For Valentine's Day, I filled little baskets with candy bars and other goodies for John and Sophie. She got the biggest smile when I handed hers to her. Peppermint Pattys were her new favorite. She laughed when she saw how many of them were in her basket. I was always happy to find something she could munch on and enjoy while John and I were at work for all those hours. I hated that I could not "make" her understand how to use the microwave, the television, the dishwasher, and something that was becoming more and more evident lately, the shower.

Our house was starting to stink. It was obvious to me that Sophie was having bladder control issues. For some reason, John could not smell anything that smelled badly. He had no trouble whatsoever smelling something good, like a roast beef in the oven or onions and garlic sautéing in butter. I suppose that was kind of a gift. I, on the other hand, am overly sensitive to bad odors. It could be frustrating at times trying to explain to him how bad our house smelled.

I asked Sophie if she wanted to go shopping with me for new underwear. I always seemed to be treating her the way I would treat a small child. I would tell her that I needed something so she would want it too. Most of the time, it worked. She wanted to go to Walmart. I told her as soon as she bathed and dressed we would go.

I told her I would start her bath. Once the water was warm and milky white with skin softener and creamy bubbles, I announced it was ready for her to get into. I had to go into her room with her to help her pick out the clothes she would put on after her bath. It would frustrate me because her room was always filthy no matter how often I cleaned up in there. She never seemed to be in the room, but it was always a mess. I noticed her bed was always made. In fact, the bed was always perfectly made.

That is one positive thing, I thought.

At least she can make a bed on her own. Then I realized that her bed was always nicely made because she wasn't sleeping in her bed. More and more nights were spent with her sleeping in the blue recliner. I planned on getting some upholstery cleaner and a few protective pads for that chair.

I thought about the people that always say God has a sense of humor. He knew what he was doing in this case for sure. Germs, smells, and dirty, lazy people just about send me into convulsions. Here I was with this germ-ridden, smelly, and very lazy elderly woman living in our home. As much as I felt we were getting to know Sophie and as much as it was starting to feel like she was just another one of our crazy relatives, there was still so much we didn't know about her. After all of these months, how was it even possible that she was still very much the stranger in our recliner?

Sophie came out of the bathroom with her hair dripping wet. It was as obvious as a flood that she did not even touch her head with a towel. The back of her shirt was soaked. The entire bathroom, hallway, and steps were now soaking wet as well. I told her to get a towel and dry her hair. It was freezing outside. There was no way she could go outside like that.

She told me her hand and arm hurt and she could not hold the towel. I ran up the steps and into the bathroom and grabbed a few towels. I started vigorously massaging her head with the towel. She shrieked and whined the whole time. I asked her if she would like me to use the hair dryer and to style her hair for her. She agreed, but again like a child, she shrieked ridiculously loud the entire time.

"It's too hot. It's burning my head. You pulling my hair," she whined.

She refused to allow me to use any clips, barrettes, or headbands. I did my best to curl it under a bit. The result was worth it. She looked "normal"—actually, better than normal. She looked pretty.

I had to run back upstairs and change my own soaking wet blouse. All of my life, I seemed to just allow people to do things to me like this. It was not okay for Sophie to get my blouse soaking wet because she was too lazy to dry her own hair. Whenever stuff like this happens, I never respond angrily. I have been told by therapists at least a dozen times that I must learn to deal with my anger in a healthy way. My healthy way was always to ignore it, take a deep breath, and move on from the infraction. It was easier for me to do things myself than to constantly nag others about what they were doing wrong. I decided it wasn't my job nor was it even possible for me to change Sophie's or anyone's behavior. The only thing I could change was my reaction, and my choice back then was not to have any reaction. I would rather be wrong and happy than right and unhappy. Unless of course someone chooses to do something that hurts someone in our family, especially our children and grandchildren. Then it is possible, even likely, that I might pull out my pen and write about them and their infraction. Journaling was the way I learned to deal with my deep hurts when I was about ten years old. It helped me to see things more clearly back then, and it still works to this day.

I finally got Sophie safely buckled into the Mustang and off we went to the Walmart. I reached up and rubbed the Mother Theresa medal dangling from my rearview mirror. I loved the medal because Mother Theresa was holding a baby wrapped in a pink blanket. It reminded me of the baby girl I lost so many years ago. The medal was given to me by an elderly client.

Please let this be a smooth, safe trip, I recited to myself over and over again. *Please don't let me be horrified by Sophie's embarrassing behaviors.*

I loved driving that Mustang. John gave it to me when we became engaged. I loved that it was a convertible, but I rarely put the top down. I never liked wind. That thought made me shake my head and smile because John had a Harley–Davidson motorcycle, and most weekends, I would happily hop on the back and ride with him. The only time the wind became unbearable was on the highways and occasionally, riding by the ocean. I suppose it was different in the Mustang with the top down because I was the one driving, so the wind truly was in my face. The interior of the car was black and tan, one of my favorite combinations. The exterior was black with a tan convertible top, and the tan pinstripes went together perfectly. John kept the car detailed and waxed for me. It was so nice to have my car taken care of after being a single mom for so many years. Sophie loved riding in the car too. She seemed to go back and forth between feeling anxious and smiling proudly whenever we rode together. She always lit up when we got to an area she was familiar with. Other areas seemed to make her cringe and sink down in the seat. I always tried to reassure her I would never ever leave her anywhere. She would always be coming home with me no matter how upset I ever got with her. Not that I didn't occasionally think about leaving her somewhere or anywhere, because I did. I am not proud of those thoughts, but I had them often.

No matter what day or time it is, the Walmart parking lot is always overcrowded. Rather than waiting until someone left a close parking spot or riding around the parking lot aimlessly looking for a spot close to the front doors, I chose to park at the very end of the aisle that was closest to the front doors. The walk would do both of us good. We might freeze to death. It was bitter cold and windy out but at least we would have some exercise, and we both needed more of that without a doubt. Sophie never seemed to complain much about the cold. I offered to drop her off at the door, but she flatly refused. We always had to remind her to put on her gloves, a scarf, and a hat. We could remind her, but she rarely listened, and she could never find them. Even though she refused being let out of the car at the front door, she complained loudly the entire walk to the front of the store.

Once we were inside the store, I asked her what she wanted to look for first and what she thought we needed in the way of food. She answered peas as she normally did.

"We have plenty of peas," I assured her. I had no doubt we would end up with more peas in our cart. I was beginning to dislike peas immensely.

I yanked on a cart that was parked in the outside corral. Why was I always the one that seemed to end up with the cart that was hopelessly stuck? I wiggled and then yanked it side to side, pushed forward, and pulled back. My hands were so cold. Just as my impatience was about to peak, the cart came loose, hitting me in the chest, nearly knocking me off of my feet. Hoping nobody saw me stumble, I asked Sophie if she wanted to push the cart. I thought she might like to lean on it for stability.

"No." That was it from her, just a simple no.

"Sophie, come to church with us on Sunday," I asked her as we walked by the men's dress shirt aisle and I scanned the ties. John wears ties to work, so I am always on the lookout for different, fun patterns. She said she would not be able to go to church because she did not have anything nice enough to wear.

"We can buy you something pretty," I assured her. "I will treat you to a nice outfit and some shoes."

"No, me don't want to go to no church," she insisted.

She went on to tell me that God does not like her. She felt that God left her alone to be treated badly by her mother and then by her siblings. He left her alone to be beaten by a drunken husband and then left her alone to sleep in the woods and to be karate chopped by Elvis's girlfriend.

I stopped the cart and looked into her sad eyes. I told her that maybe God sent John to find her that night. Maybe God knew it was too cold for her to be outside anymore at her age. I told her she was okay now. I told her it was okay if she did not want to go to church, but she should think about it because it might help her to feel better. Heck, it would definitely make me feel a lot better. Maybe if she showed up at the church, they would do something for her. I am not saying that's the way it should be because I definitely felt that was not the way it should be. She assured me it was too late for her. She was too angry with God, and going to church was not going to help her at all.

I changed the subject. "We should pick you up some new bras, underwear, socks, and maybe some new pajamas."

She said okay to the bras and underwear and no to everything else. I wondered how I would ever broach the Depend idea with her. I had to admit to myself that the Depend conversation most likely would not be happening that day. If we got her more underwear, it would help for now. I wouldn't have to do her laundry as often.

We both went about browsing in different directions in the lingerie section. I purposely stayed several racks away from her for two reasons. One of the reasons was to help her to feel and act more independent, and second, if I am being honest, was the fact that she was downright embarrassing in a store.

She would look at the price on a tag and start shouting, "Are they out of their minds, eight dollars for a pack of cheap ugwy underwear?"

I wanted to laugh and cry at the same time. I didn't feel I had any reason to be embarrassed, but my cheeks turned red with embarrassment even though my mind told them not too.

"Sophie, that is quite reasonable," I tried to assure her.

"I want to go to the dollar store," she started whining.

I grabbed two six-packs of plain-white cotton Hanes underwear and two bras that were her size and put them in the cart. She reached right in and took them out.

"Me not paying that," she yelled.

I put them back in and told her they were for me and that I would take her to the dollar store. Thank goodness she believed me. I would wash them and put them in her drawers. Hopefully, by the time they landed in her drawer, she would forget she didn't want them. Was she seriously going to buy underwear at the dollar store? How in the world would I talk her out of that? We moved on to the body wash and shampoo section of the store.

I immediately noticed a woman staring at Sophie in the hair dye aisle. She walked up beside me and asked me if that was Sophie. I nodded yes. The woman said Sophie looked great and asked if I was a relative. I started feeling defensive, and the woman must have sensed that because she quickly told me she worked at that McDonald's on Chester Pike, the one Sophie used to hang out in to get warm. She told me all of the other people that worked at that McDonald's location were wondering and worrying about what had become of Sophie. They had been so worried about her that they were riding around several neighborhoods hoping to find her. I felt guilty about that. We should have stopped in and told them she was safe. In my defense, I assumed they didn't care. Sophie joined the conversation for just a minute, acknowledging she knew the woman, and then put her head down and went back to looking at shampoo and hair dye. Sophie had been telling me for over a month that she wanted to color her hair red. Now she was complaining about the prices of the dye. I quickly told the woman that my husband and I were just trying to help Sophie and keep her off the streets.

She said, "God bless both of you," and asked me to stop by with Sophie over the holidays and she would buy us lunch. I thanked her and told her I would be happy to come by to see her and the others. The chance meeting reminded me how a few strangers made a difference for Sophie, but her own large family was nowhere to be found.

There should be a law against abandoning your *humans* similar to the law making it illegal to abandon dogs and cats. That was how the authorities were able to rescue that first child so many years ago in New York City from a life of abuse. The police were frustrated and worried that the child would be killed, so they put their heads together and filed charges based on it being illegal to abuse animals. They argued that the child was a possession and therefore deserved to be protected under the law that made it illegal to abuse horses or any animal. It worked. Because of the creativity or desperation of those cops to save one tiny little girl, it became illegal to abuse children. There are laws on the books today making it illegal to abuse the elderly too, but I'm not sure there are laws making it illegal to abandon them.

It was nice to meet someone that knew and cared about Sophie. I wished we would run into a relative of hers one day. I wished Sophie would tell me where her sisters and brothers lived. What in the world was she hiding from us? We moved on to the food section. I started selecting cans of kidney beans, diced tomatoes, and sauce. I was planning to make a big pot of chili. Sophie started yelling right there in the crowded canned food aisle in Walmart. I knew for sure we were going to make it onto one of those only in Walmart sites.

"I don't want no chili. I don't like no chili. Me telt you me hate chili."

I told her she was not allowed to have any of the chili because it was only for John and me. I told her I would make something special for her that night, whatever she wanted. What I really wanted to do was to smack her across her face and scream *shut up*! I never would actually slap her or anyone, but honestly, I wanted too.

"Why do you hate chili so much?" I asked her.

Finally, she answered the question loudly, but it was an answer.

"My sister made it when me went to her house to visit. She knew me didn't like it or want to eat chili. Me told her a million times. She always does what me doesn't want, and then she laughs. She is so mean. She is going to rot in hell for that."

"Where does she live?" I quickly asked while trying to digest the thought of being thrown into hell for making chili for dinner.

"In Newtown Square, she thinks she's somethin'."

Aha! She answered without realizing she was giving me that little tidbit of information I was desperately hoping and praying for. I filed that information in my mind for future reference, and hoping she was finished shopping, I guided Sophie to the checkout aisle.

I did not realize just how stressful that trip was until I sat back down in the car. I took a deep breath and sat back into my seat and felt my muscles slowly relax. I was so relieved it was over. There was no way I could make it through the supermarket with her on that day. I asked her if she wanted a cheeseburger.

"Double cheeseburger," she answered with a smile. "So me can save half for later."

That half of a cheeseburger would be saved in the refrigerator until it was petrified. Only then could I sneak it into the garbage can without her knowing. My refrigerator was cluttered with napkins balled up around a couple of peas, halves of bananas, and dried up pieces of bread crusts. It was gross.

I wondered how I could now get her to tell me the name of her sister in Newtown Square. If I just had a name, I could do some research and maybe find out who and where these people were and why they treated Sophie so badly.

The days seemed to be running into each other. I felt like I needed to be doing more to find a place for her, and at the same time, I was getting sick and tired of wasting my valuable, little time off chasing down and jumping through hoops to end up getting nothing accomplished. I was in serious procrastination mode.

I asked Sophie to gather up all of her important papers, social security card, access cards, birth certificate, and medical records so we could get them all organized for her. She did not rush to get the stuff together. I nudged her about it every day and told her we needed to file everything on my next day off.

Surprisingly, she produced a lot of important documents. A medical card and a bunch of banking paperwork. When I say a bunch of paperwork, I mean at least thirty pieces of paper folded in half and in half again shoved into this sort of small pocketbook-looking thing. It was the first time I caught a glimpse of what was in that ratty-looking bag of hers. As she unfolded the papers, I kid you not, rocks fell out. I wondered if I should bother asking about them. I could not help myself. She told me she kept the rocks in there so if someone tried to beat her up, she could hit them with her bag and run. All in all, the rock idea was a good theory, but these rocks were more like large pebbles, even stones, and it was all I could do to keep from laughing at her, the poor thing.

She gave up the papers to me much easier than she gave up those lousy rocks. I decided to let her keep them in her bag, and I would save that battle for another day. I could not make much sense of the papers other than it was useless, out-of-date information and junk mail sort of stuff that she was dead set against throwing away. I grabbed some file folders from my office, arranged the papers as neatly as possible, and placed the folders in one of her empty drawers. Most of Sophie's drawers were empty because she kept all of her clothes on top of the dresser. When I asked her why she didn't put them inside the drawers, she said it was because she was karate chopped and her hand hurt too much to be opening and closing drawers every morning. Her pinky and ring finger on her left hand did appear to be bent and curling up. I wondered if that was a form of arthritis or was it a result of some kind of injury. She insisted it was from the time in the storage unit that Jim the Elvis person's girlfriend beat her up.

Call me crazy, but I wholeheartedly believed *this* story of hers. She was so adamant, and it did make sense although it was senseless. I asked her again why she did not press charges against the woman. She told me the police took her to the hospital because they did not believe her story. I think the police were complacent and did what has become habit for all law enforcement. They take the most vulnerable-looking person out of the situation and drop them off at the emergency room of the closest hospital with a mental health unit. It isn't completely the police officers' fault. They have little if no resources and even less training available to them for helping the mentally ill, the addicted, and the homeless. Most all of our first responders have the biggest hearts. They have to be in order to be the ones running toward the fires and the gunshots with only thoughts of helping people and not one thought of themselves.

Are there a few bad ones? Absolutely, but the number is extremely low.

I wondered how long ago the assault in the storage unit happened. If I was figuring correctly, she lived in the woods for approximately six months, and she had now been with us going on six months. I was considering looking into pressing charges or filing a civil suit against Elvis and his new woman. I needed to find out what the statute of limitations was on this sort of assault crime. I wondered if Sophie could possibly sue the woman that worked at the storage facility that didn't help her. I knew I had no time or energy to get involved with any kind of a lawsuit, but I felt the facility, the owner, and that woman deserved to be sued.

It was hard to believe that this woman had been living with us for the past six months. It was even more unbelievable that there seemed to be little possibility she would be leaving our home any time soon. I needed to stop procrastinating and get back to working at getting her back on track and into her own home. I needed to go back to Walmart to pick her up some Depends, and then I was going to need to talk her into wearing them.

7

Wave on Wave

Every June we have a McGettigan family reunion at the Jersey shore. John and I rent a large house and all of our kids and grandkids join us for a week of fun at the seashore. John's sisters, all six of them and his younger brother along with their families are also there for the week. The tradition was started by their parents. One night Frank McGettigan came home from his work as an architect and told his wife, "I have some extra money, do you want me to save it or would you like me to build a beach house for the kids?"

Without hesitation Kathleen opted for the vacation home. John was only one year old. He spent every summer until he was eighteen years old on that beach. At eighteen he joined the Air Force.

John and I had our first date and thirteen months later we were married on that same beach during the annual family beach week. It will always be a special time and place for us and we want it to be special for our kids and grandkids as well.

That first night, our first date we were sitting on the wooden steps that led to the beach. They were covered in sand but I didn't care. My heart was beating so fast, and I felt like I couldn't catch my breath. I was scared to death and at the same time there was nowhere else I wanted to be at that moment in time. I looked up at the sky and gasped. I had never seen so many bright large stars. His hand was warm as he brushed my cheek and he moved closer. He was going to kiss me and just as his lips brushed mine the ground shook and the sky exploded loudly into brilliant colors. Scared, we scrambled to our feet. He grabbed my hands and held them tight. We had no idea where those fireworks came from. We thought the beach was deserted. We never saw anyone. A few minutes passed, we relaxed and ended up sitting on those steps and chatting the entire night away.

This is it, I thought. *The beginning of a summer love, something before now I only ever dreamed of having.*

I was living with my daughter, helping her and her husband with their newborn son and their son with special needs. The stars had finally aligned in my favor. I was able to make a break from an abusive relationship.

Once I settled into my new surroundings, my girls decided I should do some online dating. It was more like they were going to do it for me. You see, my picker was broken. I lacked the ability to pick myself a good guy.

I learned a lot during my thirteen months of online dating. I felt the way I always imagined a teenager felt. I was out five nights a week, usually with a different guy each night. I became an expert at sneaking into the house at dawn and not waking the kids.

Having been married at sixteen, a mother at seventeen, divorced in my twenties, and then a single mom into my forties I never had the opportunity to know what it was like to *act* like a teenager. I certainly did make up for lost time.

After thirteen months I decided to take a break from my dating escapades and devote my free time to writing a book, something I always wanted to do. My dating break was short lived.

When the girls first showed me his picture my gut reaction was, "Oh hell no!"

This guy was leaning on a motorcycle and he was wearing a wifebeater. His pickup line was, "I see you love to cook and I love to eat. I think we will get along great."

I wanted to laugh but my daughter said to look at his eyes. He wore a smile but his eyes told a sad story.

We e-mailed, texted like teens and then graduated to phone conversations. We both agreed it was finally time to meet.

My daughter and I went shopping for a new outfit. It was May twentieth but still a bit chilly in the Philadelphia area. I picked out a soft spring-colored sweater. I was giddy, a foreign feeling for the usually in-total-control me.

When we left the restaurant the sun was still shining bright. I wondered if he was going to try to kiss me when he said good-bye. Instead, he asked me to take a ride down the shore with him. I had butterflies in my stomach and felt a bit dizzy. I wanted to say yes, but what if he was an axe murderer? The shore was pretty much deserted that time of the year and there had been shark sightings. Why did I watch so many episodes of *Forensic Files* the night before?

I looked up at the dashboard of his truck and saw a little stuffed Winnie-the-Pooh and blurted out, "Yes, I will go to the seashore with you!" No murderer would ever have a Winnie-the-Pooh beanie baby on his dashboard.

My first summer love and I were married thirteen months later on that very beach where we shared our first kiss on our first date surrounded by and supported by our families.

Now, along with that Winnie-the-Pooh beanie baby still on the dashboard, three trucks later, we ride down the shore as often as we can just to sit on those wooden steps for a few minutes. We hold hands and look up at the sky to see all of the brilliant possibilities still ahead of us. Taking in a homeless elderly woman is one possibility we never considered but it is now woven into our life story, and it is what it is. Neither John nor I believed in coincidences, so we both knew Sophie was in our lives for a reason.

We started to wonder how Sophie would react to being at the shore with all of us. She did not do well in crowds and our bunch all together was quite a crowd. I thought the change of scenery would do wonders for her. My only issues with her being on vacation with us would be the way she depended on me for everything and her odor. I needed to find a way to get her to take care of herself. I tried leaving notes for her with step-by-step instructions on operating the microwave, the TV remote and reminders to get washed and dressed. It didn't work. I was convinced she had no interest whatsoever in helping herself. I was caught somewhere between wanting to coddle her and wanting to scream at her.

"Get up and do something with your life."

We decided we would start talking about the trip in front of her to see how she would react. At first she loved the idea and seemed excited about going with us. She asked if she could have her own room and asked if she could eat garlic and onions and then sit in the ocean so we didn't have to smell her. We said yes to both and with that, Sophie was going to be joining our family on vacation. I was looking forward to seeing her reaction to the beach. It would be good for her. The ocean is good for everyone's soul. Hopefully she would be able to relax and have some fun. Would she really want to sit in the ocean and eat onions and garlic raw? If it made her happy I would buy them for her. The kids would probably get a big kick out of watching her. I hoped the ocean would wash away the smell.

A few days later while John was at work, Sophie asked me if she could stay home at our house while we went to the shore. I was so disappointed. Who wouldn't want to go to the beach for a week? She wanted me to get her a bunch of fresh garlic and onion and she was going to eat it while we were gone. She said that way we would not have to smell her and the smell would be gone from the house by the time we got home. She caught me completely off guard and I had no idea what to say.

"Why would you ever want to do that to yourself?" I asked her.

"Because it cures cancer," she told me.

Without a pause, I asked her if she had cancer. She quickly answered no and shook her head back and forth.

"I don't got no cancer. It keeps me from getting it and it really does. I saw it on TV. Me can take care of the dogs too," she continued. "They don't want to go to no beach. It will burn their little feet."

It took a lot for me to get excited about her going on vacation with us. I was so disappointed that she wasn't excited about going and the fact that I was disappointed that she didn't want to go surprised me. Then I wondered what she was up to.

I told her I would ask John if it would be okay for her to stay home alone. I also told her I would be happy to get her onions and garlic and she could eat small amounts every day. I assured her it wouldn't be so smelly that way. I tried to convince her that I use a lot of onion and garlic when I cook and told her we will start eating more broccoli and other foods that contain antioxidants. It would help all of us, I tried to assure her. She did not believe that broccoli was one of the foods that could prevent cancer and she also did not believe that cooked onions and garlic also worked. I had to prove to her that yes, broccoli was indeed also an antioxidant and did help to prevent cancer and cooked onion and garlic were still good for you. I'm not sure I convinced her but she did start eating more broccoli—we all did.

Did she have cancer? A strong voice from deep in my gut was telling me I needed to get her to the doctor, to her doctor and soon. He needed to give me some answers. I prayed I wasn't right but something told me Sophie was sick.

Although arrangements were made for several neighbors to check on her and the dogs while we were away I continued to try convincing her to come along with us. I thought the change would be so good for her. She adamantly refused. I got the feeling she had ulterior motives for not wanting to go. I couldn't figure out what they would be. My imagination ran wild.

I left the fridge full of fresh chopped up garlic, onions, broccoli, and carrots. I prepared and wrapped a lunch and dinner for each day we would be gone. On the pantry shelf I left several boxes of cereal, cookies, and crackers. I left extra treats for the dogs and went over and over again with her on the proper amounts of food and treats and the times to feed them. One of our neighbors promised to stop in as often as he could during the times the dogs were supposed to eat.

We had the greatest time with the kids but wondering and worrying about what was going on in our home was never far from my mind. John called often to check in and continued to assure me all was well at home.

When we returned I was surprised and frustrated at the same time that none of the food I spent hours carefully planning and preparing had so much as been touched. In fact she did not eat any of the food I left for her. She did not take one bite of anything. Our generous neighbors brought platters over for her the entire time we were gone and that was all she ate.

"Me did eat some of me garwic," she insisted when I asked her why she didn't even touch the stuff. It wasn't touched.

I was still too Zen from our whirlwind vacation but that was quickly starting to wear off. It was starting to feel more like a beautiful dream I was just waking up from. I wasn't going to let Sophie or anyone bring me down. I just shrugged it off. I simply threw away whatever food was bad or close to it and rewrapped what was salvageable.

I was wondering if her speech was affected by her lack of teeth. I finally got my nerve up and asked her why she never got dentures. She told me a rotten dentist in Upper Darby took all of her teeth out for no reason. She insisted there was nothing wrong with any of them and she was never going back to that dentist again. I asked if she would like to see a nicer dentist if I could find one for her. She said she would like that. I didn't believe any dentist would take her teeth out for no reason. I do know that Medicaid will not pay for a lot of dental treatments or any cosmetic treatments. This leaves patients who have several front teeth that need work with no choice but to opt for dentures. This is most likely what happened with Sophie. Perhaps the dentist wasn't the best, and he didn't create comfortable dentures for her. Or maybe she didn't cooperate during the sizing phase of treatment.

I could not find a dentist to take her Medicaid insurance. I told her she should save some money and then she should buy herself some brand-new teeth. I told her she could get the best teeth available if she bought them herself. She seemed excited by the idea of implants once I explained what they were and said she would start saving right away. I needed to find a dentist for John and myself too. I promised her we would go with her and we would have work done too.

We spent the rest of that summer cheering on the Phillies from our living room on the big red sofa, Sophie in the blue recliner and the grandkids sprawled out on blankets and pillows on the floor. I didn't have enough rally towels to go around so we gave those to the kids and Sophie. John and I used white washcloths. With the bases loaded, two outs and Ryan Howard up to bat we would all be on our feet jumping up and down screaming and waving those white cloths over our heads. I glanced over and looked at Sophie to see a big smile not only on her face but in her eyes. Her hand was up over her head and she was swinging that towel with everything she had. I glanced down at the floor and there were the kids jumping, screaming, smiling, and waving their towels. Standing next to me was my husband and best friend shouting and praying at the same time. For me, during those few precious moments in my living room, time always seemed to stop, giving me a few minutes to catch my breath and feel pure, honest joy.

We have our baseball watching traditions and most of them include Phillies snacks like hotdogs, popcorn, and ice cream. Other traditions we have are of course to wear our favorite player's jerseys and to have our rally towels in our hands. We were so proud of Sophie when she remembered the players' names and we were especially proud when she *finally* learned the rules of the game and started to yell at the umpires.

Of course as often as we could John and I were cheering from the stands hoping for another World Series and a championship. We wanted to take Sophie to a game but she would not agree to go with us. I felt like she believed we would leave her there or anywhere we had the chance to and the thought that she had to live with the fear and torture of that thought was heartbreaking for me. I wished I could convince her that she had nothing to be afraid of when she was with us. She told me she didn't feel that way but why else would she be so adamant about not going to any place that might be overly crowded and some distance from the house?

8

Crash

I have never been a fan of the fall. It is not so much that I
don't like the season of falling and wet leaves. The weather is
always so gorgeous in the northeast. I enjoy the flavors of fall
especially anything pumpkin flavored. I just do not like the idea
of summer ending. The older I was getting the more profound
the changes in season seemed to become and the tougher it
was getting to deal with any change at all. I did not like feeling
so old that life's changes affected me so profoundly. I think I
would have preferred if life could slow down a bit. My out-
of-the-house job was getting to me. The hours were long and
it was depressing to be with someone twelve hours a day that
wanted nothing more than to die when I wanted nothing more
than to live.

That September, that client finally got what she wanted. I
was with her for a long time. I felt so sad that she didn't die
happy but had to realize my happy was quite different from her
happy. I will never forget her three sons, their spouses, and her
grandchildren surrounding her bed and holding hands. They
sang song after song and it brought tears to my eyes. She must
have been waiting for them to all be together. She passed away

quietly the next morning. Her funeral was a joyful celebration of her life in better times.

I knew I would have a few weeks to relax before the company would send me a new client. This would be a great time to have some extra visits with my grandkids. Cleaning out Sophie's room and some other neglected areas of the house would hopefully make me feel better. It would also free up some time for me to get some serious writing done. That is if I could find a way to occupy Sophie.

I received the news that my oldest nephew would be attending school at Widener University which was only about fifteen minutes from our house. He was a football player and I was looking forward to his games as well as having other family members visit our home. For a change maybe the changes this fall were something to look forward to.

If I was going to be having company I definitely had to clean the house. We put up with the stink of Sophie for too long. I needed to get to the bottom of and solve the odor problem.

My motivation was on overdrive. I cleaned and sanitized every inch of the house including Sophie's room and bathroom. She was not happy about the scrubbing of that recliner and I am still sickened when I think of the melted Peppermint Patty bars stuck to *Soap Opera Digest* magazines. She mumbled quietly as she sat on the big red sofa and watched me flutter around the house with my Swiffer and my bucket of Pine-Sol for days. She did not lift one finger to help.

I was immensely proud of my nephew and was enjoying spending Saturday afternoon at the Widener football field watching him play. It was so much fun sitting in those stands with my younger nieces and nephew too.

On the last Saturday morning of the month my boss called and asked if I would go meet with and care for a new client for just a few hours early that evening. She explained the woman had some frontal lobe damage (which meant nothing to me at the time). The husband had been taking care of her but wanted to do some socializing with friends. My boss told me the woman was forgetful and had to be watched carefully so she did not wander off.

I asked Sophie if she wanted to come to the game with me. It was such a warm day and she never went out for fresh air. I could not convince her to go.

I ended up leaving the game a bit early because I wanted to stop home and fix Sophie some dinner before I went to work. She was so mad when I reminded her I had to go to work. She wanted me to sit and watch the soap channel with her until John got home. I created a soap opera monster. She was watching every single show. Most days she watched each episode at least twice if not three times. She loved when I bought her any kind of soap opera magazine or newspaper. I got a kick out of how into the characters she was. She acted as though it was reality TV. She loved Katherine Chancellor and despised Jill. Silly me, I encouraged her because I thought it was good that she enjoyed *something* so much and it was inspiring her to read. I gave her other books to read but she was never interested. She preferred magazines.

I explained to her that we needed the money so I had to go to work and I assured her John would be home shortly. She suggested she could give me money and then I could stay home with her all the time. I scared myself by actually considering the offer before quickly shaking it off as a moment of insanity. After all I did go out of the house to care for elderly people who were home alone. I shook it off again. It was not a good idea. The idea of my job was to get me out of the house occasionally. When I spent all of my time at home writing, there were some days I didn't even get dressed. The days would run into each other.

Getting out of the house was good for my creativity and my sanity. Not to mention I loved my job. I enjoyed helping people.

The inside of my Mustang was hot I had to roll the windows down for a few minutes to give the air-conditioning a chance to get cool. It took a few minutes for my GPS to wake up. Maggie (Magellan) must have gotten too warm. I typed in the address the office gave to me for my new client and was relieved that it was only eighteen minutes away. I hated feeling rushed and even worse being late.

I put on my seatbelt, turned on WXTU, our local country music station and pulled away from the house. I drove slowly because there were so many little kids out and about in the neighborhood. Some were riding their bikes on the sidewalk. One five-year-old little boy was riding in the street. He always did. I was so scared that he would be hit by a car. All of the neighbors watched out for him because his parents didn't. There were other people walking dogs and the bigger kids were playing football in the street. They were the ones that scared me the most. They have no fear or any manners to speak of for that matter. Was I getting that old that a bunch of kids made me crabby?

I put on my blinker and proceeded to make a left turn and was slammed into on the passenger side of my car by a very large red car. I was shaking and felt like I couldn't catch my breath. I felt a crushing pain in my right hand and a sharp pain shooting up my right arm and another sharp shooting pain running down my left leg. I was dizzy. I reached for my cell phone. As I picked up my phone from the console, at my driver's side window appeared this large young woman. She was banging on my window and screaming for me to get out of the car. Trembling and trying to put two thoughts together, I dialed 911 as she continued screaming and banging on my window. Luckily the police station was located at the other end of that street. An officer was there in less than two minutes. When she saw the officer approaching, she ran to her car and drove down to the stop sign which wasn't very far. She was going to take off but must have decided against that foolish move. Thank God she didn't take off, I remembered thinking. I didn't want her speeding down the street where the kids were playing. She parked against the curb but stayed in her car.

I called my boss to tell her about the accident and told her I was okay and would still be able to make it to the clients house but I may be a half hour or so late. Then I called my husband. I assured him I was okay and would be going to work. What was I thinking? He asked about the car. I shook my head a little and got out to go look at the car. I expected to see the whole passenger side smashed. The red car hit right on the back tire. The dent wasn't that bad. I took a deep breath and was so relieved. I loved that car. It was an engagement gift from my husband. It was the first time in more than twenty years I wasn't driving a station wagon or a minivan.

The officer asked me if the red car ran the stop sign. I said, "Yes, she was going too fast to avoid hitting me."

He had us both sit in our own cars. He took my information and then went to get hers. My husband called and I spoke with him until the officer came back. He informed me he would have an accident report ready on Monday afternoon and I could come to the station to pick it up then. I thanked him and drove away. I heard a slight rubbing sound coming from that back tire.

I was not expecting that freak neighborhood accident, not that anyone would ever expect such a thing. It was completely out of place on such a gorgeous fall day. I struggled to concentrate on the directions coming from my GPS.

Appropriately the sky darkened and it started to drizzle.

By the time I arrived at the client's house it was pouring. I arrived at the front door looking like a drowned rat. The man could not have been nicer. He got me a towel and asked if I was okay. The company informed him of the accident and told him I would be arriving late.

He introduced me to his wife and together they showed me around their beautiful house. She did not say one word. I felt her eyes. I was trying to gauge if she was feeling nervous or if she was angry. The husband left me his cell number and assured me he would be gone at the most three hours. He was going to have dinner and a few drinks with friends.

Once he left the woman and I went into a sunroom where she sat on a sofa and I sat on a chair. Their home was gorgeous and the property went on forever and looked beautifully landscaped even with the downpour. The sunroom was large, the size of an average living room with windows on all sides except where it was connected to the house. I wondered if deer and other animals ran around on the property.

I asked her if she wanted a snack and she said yes. We went into the kitchen and I filled a paper plate with Doritos and then got her a can of ginger ale from the refrigerator. I made a cup of hot tea for myself. She did not take her eyes off me for a second. I was feeling tense. The two of us went into yet another room, this one a den. Most elderly people in this area enjoyed watching baseball. Our Phillies were doing exceptionally well. I asked her if she wanted to watch the game and she smiled and said yes. It took me a few minutes to figure out their cable system but I was determined. It was such a relief to find the game. I settled back into an overstuffed sofa, feeling relieved that this might be an easy shift after all.

It was going very well. We chatted very little. She wasn't interested in me other than the random dirty looks she shot my way. We just sat there watching the game eyeing each other occasionally. I should have known it was too good to be true.

She got up from the sofa and bolted to the front door and then out onto the front porch. It was dark and it was still pouring.

Oh dear God, I thought, *what was I going to do now?* It took all of my strength to hold onto her to keep her from running off into the road. I somehow convinced her to get back inside the house and I was relieved to get the door locked.

She sat down for a few minutes and just when I felt comfortable again she darted for the front door. I got there first and struggled to keep her from opening the door. I looked up and noticed there was a hidden latch at the top of the door.

I was so grateful. I knew it was a safety feature to keep her inside. Why hadn't her husband told me to keep the latch on the door? I wondered. I was able to get her to look away for a second and when she did I reached up and slid the latch into the lock position.

Once she realized she could not get that door open, she ran into her bedroom and slammed the door. Thank goodness there was no lock on that door. She did have her body against the door and was not about to let me into that room. I knew I had to calm myself down first if I was going to have any chance to calm her down and get her to open that door. She was obviously frightened of me. I decided to just sit outside the door quietly and let her calm herself down. I looked down and noticed my hands were scratched and bleeding. They stung. There was a bathroom directly in front of me. I walked in there as softly as I could and ran the cold water, dampened a paper towel and wiped away the blood.

She appeared in the doorway and started accusing me of wanting her husband and her house. I tried as hard as I could to convince her I had my own husband, I loved him very much, we had our own house and we even had an elderly woman living with us. She stopped trying to pull me out of the bathroom and with glazed over eyes, she just stared. I spoke to her as softly as I could. I told her about Sophie and my husband and how beautiful our house was. I told her about Lance and Louie, our cute but mischievous little dogs. Reaching slowly for my purse I took out my wallet and showed her pictures of my grandchildren. She was not interested. I showed her my arms and quietly told her how wrong it was for her to hurt me like that when I was only there to help her. I told her I would be happy to be her girlfriend and if she wanted to vent about her husband and her fears I would be happy to listen.

She attempted two more mad dashes for the door but settled down much easier once she realized she could not get the door open. She continued to accuse me of all sorts of things—stealing her jewelry, her kids, and her clothes. I was so relieved to hear her husband's car pull into the garage. I gave him a quick version of what transpired while he was gone and showed him my arms. He looked devastated. I knew he was hoping for a break a couple of times a week. He realized that was not going to happen.

I called my supervisor as soon as I got into the car. I had never turned down a difficult client but I was not up for this challenge. I never like the idea of taking someone from the home and placing them in a facility. In this case it seemed necessary for her safety. I felt sad for both of them. Once I looked up frontal lobe damage which was what she had I was convinced that woman needed to be placed for her own safety, as well as her family's safety and sanity.

My amazing husband had a hot bath waiting for me along with a steaming cup of hot tea and some Advil. I love that man.

When I got up the next morning I was stiff. I didn't think much of it after the accident and the night I had. I had some breakfast and took more Advil. We decided to stay in and take it easy. I napped on and off throughout the day and each time I woke I felt more and more sore.

On Monday although I was still very sore I went back to work on the house. I started vacuuming cobwebs from our basement.

As I was sucking up the spiders and their webs, I wondered if Sophie was indeed an actual card carrying alcoholic. She never wanted to go to meetings with John. I was having serious doubts.

9

The Ceiling Is Falling

The insanity around the house continued as I single-handedly ripped down a dropped ceiling in our living room, dining room, stairway, and upstairs hallway. Sophie sat in that darn blue recliner holding the top of her head and screaming that I was making the ceiling fall on top of her head.

"Deena, you gonna make the house fall down and kill us," she screeched.

Not once did any piece of dust let alone any ceiling pieces come anywhere near her. I took care to insure she was in no danger of any injury. When I needed to do the section over her recliner she refused to move. I tried bribing her with peas, candy, soap opera magazines, and raw onions and garlic. When that didn't work I tried getting tough with her, telling her I was going to call John and that didn't work either. Finally I just slid the recliner with her in it across the room. She wailed at the top of her lungs the entire time I was sliding her. Once I could no longer take the shrieking, I told her to be quiet or I was going to tell John. To my utter surprise that worked and she pouted but remained quiet. She truly was like a two-year-old child at times.

I moved on to removing some paneling from the stairwell. The glue that held it on for thirty years was ridiculous. Chemicals were not helpful in removing it, so I had no choice but to scrape it and sand the wall. It was a long dusty process. John was so upset and kept trying to get me to slow down and let him hire someone to finish the work. Sophie moaned and/or yelled at me for most of the time that John was not home. For some reason, she was on her best behavior only when he was home. She would tell him how nicely I took care of her, what good foods I prepared for her throughout the day, and what a good job and how hard I was working on the ceiling. As soon as he was gone though, she started her whining and yelling at me all over again. For the most part I ignored her. I was on a mission to get this house in shape before going back to work and that day could not come soon enough.

I eventually ran out of energy. I was still experiencing migraines and having trouble concentrating. Reluctantly, I agreed to allow John to hire painters and let them come in to finish the job. Sophie was out of control when the painters arrived. It was so embarrassing. I did feel tiny twinges of sorry for her, trying to understand her fear of any kind of change, but mostly I was frustrated and wished she would be quiet.

She was not under any circumstances going to get out of that chair for the painters, a father-and-son team. I was so grateful that the two of them did their best to understand her, and most importantly they had great sense of humor. They continuously tried to get her to smile. They did the same thing I did and just slid her sitting in the chair from one side of the room to the other. She shrieked the whole time.

"They are killin' me. It stinks. Wahhh. Me want to hear my soaps."

Those guys did a horrible job painting our home. I think they just wanted to get away from Sophie's shrieking. They had some serious patience and were nice to Sophie.

I needed a break from the frantic pace I was keeping at home and from Sophie's whining so I decided to take a ride to my daughter's house. She lives twenty-six miles north of Philadelphia in Bristol. Bristol is a quaint, working-class river town. I bought my first house there more than thirty years ago. I raised my kids there and they all still lived there. They are now raising my grandchildren there. Whenever I'm there, I feel like I am home.

I preferred country music or talk radio while driving. Today it was all about country. The songs were good and they kept coming. Alan Jackson, Kenny Chesney, Brad Paisley, and Taylor Swift sang me on my way. I don't sing out loud because I cannot sing. I don't sing out loud in the car, the shower or anywhere—ever. When my grandson Dominic was a toddler, I was singing along with Bruce Springsteen's Christmas album, and he looked up and asked me if I would just move my mouth and not sing out loud. Like the saying out of the mouth of babes, the kid was being honest. So I took the little guy's advice and now I only sing in my mind unless I am trying to make the kids laugh.

I glanced up and noticed a sign for New York. I got an *uh-oh* feeling that felt like I was being slammed in my stomach by a two-by-four. I pulled the car over. I was nearing Newark, New Jersey. I knew where I was but had no idea why I was there or how I got there. I was shaking uncontrollably and sweating. I sat there on the side of the highway for a few minutes and prayed for my senses to return. I decided there was no way to make sense of this at the time. After a few minutes, I was feeling calmer and in complete control so I rolled back onto the highway, got off at the next exit and found the entrance back onto I-95 heading south. An hour and fifteen minutes later, I walked nonchalantly into my daughter's living room.

"You must have run into a lot of traffic." She gave me a suspecting look.

111

"It was awful," I answered and went in to talk to my grandson.

I do not know how to explain what was happening. In my mind, I knew something was wrong but I talked myself out of it quickly and moved on to another thought. My mind would not focus on the *Something is seriously wrong with me* part, and I could not force it to figure out what was wrong or to stay with the thought long enough for it to process into any sort of reasoning. As soon as I went on to the next thought the feeling of panic dissipated.

It was four days since the accident and I had not slept since it happened. I would lie in bed and toss and turn the entire night. I ached all over. I previously had a back injury and I wanted nothing to do with another injury that took years to recover from. I was wishing my neck and arm discomfort away. If I ignored them long enough, they would go away.

When I got home from my daughter's that night, I told John I thought something was wrong and I couldn't explain to him exactly what it was. The next morning we went to the emergency room at Springfield Hospital. They did x-rays of my back and neck. They asked me if I lost consciousness in the accident. I told them I couldn't remember. I was sure I did for a few seconds but I couldn't be sure. They did not x-ray or order any tests on my head.

They assured me nothing was broken. I had a contusion on my hand, whiplash, and a sprained wrist. They gave me a prescription for pain medication and told me if I wasn't feeling better in a few days to see an orthopedic doctor.

After making sure I was comfortable at home, John went to work. I fell asleep on the big red sofa and woke up hours later with a crushing headache. I made myself a cup of tea and forced down a sandwich. Sophie looked confused. Why wouldn't she be confused? Falling asleep in the middle of the day on the sofa was not something I ever did. When the food and caffeine didn't relieve my headache, I decided to try taking the pain medication the emergency room doctor prescribed. Within a half hour, I had relief from the pain so I decided to clean the kitchen. Sophie didn't say much, and honestly, I was feeling a bit resentful toward her. It would have been nice if she would have at least attempted to load the dishwasher. Something as simple as having her make me a cup of tea would have meant the world to me. I reminded myself it wasn't her fault or was it her fault?

Four hours later the crushing pain in my head was back along with arm and neck pain. I took another pain pill. Within minutes, I felt an itching sort of tingling in the back of my throat. I ran upstairs and grabbed a bottle of Benadryl from the medicine cabinet, struggled with the childproof lid and took a swig right from the bottle. I yelled for Sophie to help me find my phone. She looked at me with her head tilted. I thought I saw fear in her eyes and it made me feel bad. Calmly, I told her I was having an allergic reaction and I was going to need some help but I would be okay. As I spoke with the 911 operator, I was having trouble catching my breath. Sophie did spring into action. She found my jacket and placed it across my chest because I was shaking uncontrollably.

She kept saying, "You be okay, Deena, don't worry. They coming to help you."

Knowing I was starting to have trouble talking, I dialed John's cell phone number and handed the phone to Sophie and told her to tell John they were taking me to Crozer Hospital. He insisted on speaking with me. My tongue was so swollen I could only mumble. I felt myself losing consciousness as the EMT workers appeared at the front door. The door was locked. Sophie was not budging. I struggled to stand up. I was not going to die there with first responders on the other side of my front door. Once she saw I was on my feet Sophie jumped up and opened the door. She later told me she was scared of the police officers that appeared at the door with the EMTs.

I woke up in the emergency room feeling like I had ice water in my veins. Epinephrine, the medication used to counter allergic reactions always gives me that internal icy feeling. It was so frustrating not knowing what, when, or where these reactions could happen. One simple manufacturing change such as changing the color of the pill can put me at risk of a serious reaction. I was so relieved when John arrived. Just seeing him relieved my fear and anxiety.

A few days later, I was in an orthopedic doctor's office. This doctor was a friend of John's and he agreed to see me immediately. He was convinced I had a nasty case of whiplash and suggested I see a physical therapist. The therapist was nice but distracted. He would tell me to do several exercises and then he would go onto another patient. He told me when I finished my exercises to meet him up front. I would completely forget what he wanted me to do. I would look around and try to mimic what everyone else was doing. On my third day of physical therapy, I broke down in tears and said I couldn't do it anymore.

I went in to see my primary doctor and asked him if he could please figure out what was wrong with me. He suggested I see a neurologist. I went home and started calling the names on the list his assistant provided. One after the other, office assistants told me their practice did not see automobile accident patients. When I finally got to one on the list that did see accident victims, the earliest appointment I could schedule was for December. I was scared. I knew I would never be able to keep it together until then but I had no choice.

A woman in one of the offices I had called promised to call me if they had a cancellation. When she called a week later, I was so relieved. I saw that neurologist the following week and I could not remember why I was there. He diagnosed me with postconcussive syndrome. The symptoms were headache, memory loss, insomnia or sleeping too much, neck pain, excessive energy, excessive strength and cognitive difficulty. I had no idea what the diagnosis meant or how serious it was but I was relieved to know there was a name for what was wrong with me. The doctor told me not to drive until he cleared me. His assistant signed me up for concussion therapy. I had no idea what concussion therapy was. I hoped it wasn't as bad as my experience was with physical therapy. I felt myself becoming depressed more every day and it scared me. I had been down that dark hole before and the thought of going back there terrified me.

I wondered how it was possible to be so happy and so sad all at the same time. I loved my husband and my family but I missed my brother all the time. Now I was missing Kathleen too. We may not have been together very long but I did care for her twenty-four hours a day, seven days a week for an entire year. I struggled with focusing on the happy in my life and keeping my sadness at bay.

Concussion therapy at Mercy Fitzgerald Hospital was not fun at all. The purpose of this type of therapy is to make you dizzy and then they attempt to teach you coping methods so you can function while being dizzy. I tried to make it make sense to me.

The exercises made me nauseas. They also gave me terrible headaches. As sick to my stomach as I felt, I did my best to concentrate and listen to and do everything they asked of me. I had no choice but to believe they knew what they were doing and I desperately needed to stop feeling dizzy.

I went three times a week—Monday, Wednesday, and Friday. John had to drive me, so he went to work on those days a little later. When I returned home from these sessions, I was useless and could barely hold my head up. It was difficult to do something as simple as feeding Sophie and I. The home exercises they gave me to do kept me dizzy on Tuesdays and Thursdays. I was determined to do whatever it took to put this head injury behind me. I did give myself a break from the crazy exercises on the weekends.

Sophie was sweet to me the whole time I was sick. I was finally starting to believe that underneath her crassness, she really was a warmhearted woman. She started to tell us she loved us and we told her we loved her too. Her life circumstances may have hardened her around the edges but I was beginning to see her trust me. She was smiling more when it was just the two of us and she was starting to look like she felt more comfortable with me. It was nice not to always feel on edge when we were alone. I started to feel less and less afraid of her.

This crazy woman, the stranger in my recliner had been in our house for an entire year. As good as it felt to do something so profound for a total stranger, at the same time, the whole situation infuriated me. How dare this woman's family and her own children shrug their responsibilities off and dump their moral responsibilities off on my husband and me. It wasn't only John and I that were affected by Sophie being in our lives but our entire family was affected by her presence. Not that we were all affected in a bad way because it wasn't all bad. The saying that you never know what you are capable of until you are in a situation where you have no choice but to be capable is so true.

We hear stories of women who when their children are in extreme danger suddenly gain enormous physical strength and are able to save their children. Women who are in labor experience the most intense pain yet they find the strength to go on and give birth. You wonder how a parent could possibly continue to live on after losing a child and I look at my husband and realize he had no choice but to go on for the sake of his other son.

I wondered how it was possible for that year to have gone by and I found myself not one inch closer to finding out who this woman really was and where she came from. I was angry with myself because I wasn't working harder to get her out of our house. I had to ask myself why I wasn't making any progress in getting her out of our home. I knew the answer.

It was a feeling I first experienced while caring for my dear mother-in-law. The feeling was a sort of possessiveness of her and her care. I spent most of my days and nights caring for her by myself. I knew I was giving her 100 percent and I felt like what I was doing was the best for her. I would get upset when family members would visit and suggest I handle some portion of her care differently. I knew they loved her with all of their hearts and just wanted what was best for her and they wanted to be included in making her comfortable and happy. Selfishly, I believed nobody knew better than I did when it came to her care.

I also experienced these feelings with my elderly clients. Most family members are loving, kind, and supportive toward their elderly loved one and the caregivers. Some however would stop by maybe once a week at the most. When the client took a turn for the worst, the family members would suddenly appear and profess to know exactly what their loved one wanted and needed. The fact was, I knew exactly what my clients wanted and needed because I asked them and what they wanted never seemed to jive with what their family members wanted for them. It is a strange catch-22 sort of feeling and not being able to speak up on behalf of my clients always made me sad.

Now I was having these strong feelings about Sophie. No one would ever be able to care for her the way I do. Who would ever put up with her acting out, her dirtiness, and her laziness? I wanted her kids to come and get her and to take responsibility for her but I was starting to doubt anyone could take care of her the way I could.

There are more than thirty-four million unpaid care-givers in the United States that are caring for someone eighteen years old or older that are ill, elderly, or have a disability. Ninety percent of these caregivers are relatives, closely followed by friends and neighbors. Being cared for by strangers, like John and I, was not on any stat list anywhere.

More than half of those caregivers end up ignoring their own health because of either time or financial constraints. They also spend more than five thousand dollars a year out of their own pockets and most reduce their work hours or quit their jobs all together to keep their loved one safe.

They have trouble balancing time with family, work responsibilities and taking time for themselves. They don't accept help with care because they become convinced nobody can provide the care that they can provide.

This is where I was with Sophie. It became embarrassing for me to explain who Sophie was and where she came from to people. Sometimes I said she was John's aunt or my grandmother. I made excuses for still having her in our house and for my failure in succeeding to reunite her with her own family or at least finding a safe place for her to live. I was not taking care of myself. I was giving up or putting off things I loved to do because I was taking care of her. I told myself that once we found a safe place for her, I would have plenty of time for me. At the time, I did not recognize it was happening. I only knew that John and I were the only ones that cared enough about her to take her in and keep her safe, so we were also the ones that had no choice but to take care of her.

10

Finding Family or Not

One afternoon while Sophie was sitting in the blue recliner and I was sitting on the big red sofa, out of the corner of my eye I saw a stranger, a man approaching the house. I looked over at Sophie. From the terrified look on her face, I immediately knew she recognized him.

"Is he bad?" I asked her.

Was this her husband or her ex-husband? She got up off the chair and moved toward the door faster than I had ever seen her move and opened the door. I was screaming at her not to open the door while she screamed at the man to go away.

"Don't come here no more," she yelled to him. He got as close as the screen door and I heard Sophie whispering to him. I couldn't hear what she was saying. I was terrified, frozen on the sofa. Thankfully he listened to her and walked back down the street. I peered out the window and watched as he got into a pickup and drove away. It happened quickly and was so dramatic that immediately after he left, I felt overwhelmingly stupid. I should have opened the door and asked him a few questions. Was he one of her sons? He just caught me off guard. I wondered how he found us. I pressed Sophie to tell me who he was. How did he know she was staying here? She would only admit she knew him and that he had not been to our house before that day and he was not going to hurt her or us.

"He my friend," she said.

I felt even more stupid. He was a good person according to Sophie and because I overreacted, he probably thought I was some kind of a lunatic. How would I ever find out who he was? I was so angry with myself.

John occasionally went to the meeting place where he originally met Sophie. Without letting on that she was safe and living with us, he started to ask questions about her. Everybody seemed to know who she was and everybody had something to share about her. Not only did many people have a story to tell about her but their stories all reflected well on Sophie. Apparently she would go into the corner bar across the street from the twelve-step meeting hall and recruit the serious, as well as the occasional drinkers for the sober club. The owner of the bar asked her to stop stealing his best-paying customers and he was serious. There was also one story after another of how she showed up in court to vouch for people that had fallen off of the wagon and gotten DUIs, or worse. Sophie would appear as a character witness and then take the offender under her wing. Living off only a small pension and social security, she was the first to give you her last dollar if you needed one. Over the years when she did have a home of her own, she would take in one person after another, people that found themselves down on their luck for whatever reason. Sophie didn't judge many people so the few that she did judge, I had no choice but to assume she had a good reason.

Most likely the conversations John was having at those meetings were how Bob, the man that came to our house that day, figured out exactly where Sophie was staying. It was only a matter of time before other people would put two and two together and realize she was living with us and where we lived. If we were ever going to get any information it was a chance he felt we had to take. We felt much better about taking the risk after realizing Sophie did have a lot of friends out there.

John approached Bob and asked him how he knew Sophie. He told John he first met her in 1969. He tried to help her many times over the years. He moved her belongings with his truck numerous times. He helped her arrange for and then helped her move furniture and other belongings into storage.

Mainly he said, "I've just tried to be a friend to her. She was always nice to me, so I just wanted to help her."

John felt he was sincere and did care about Sophie. He told Bob he was welcome to come to the house to visit her any time he wanted to but asked him to keep Sophie's whereabouts to himself for now.

When Bob was nineteen years old, he walked into a bar called the Wagon Wheel in Darby, Pennsylvania. Out of the corner of his eye, he noticed a beautiful, sexy blonde woman sitting at a table.

"Sophie was so hot, a bit older than me but just gorgeous," Bob said. "I enjoyed talking with and getting to know her, and the bartenders in that bar served everyone, even those under twenty-one."

Life went on and Bob got married and then moved to Chester, Pennsylvania. He lost touch with Sophie. Twenty years later he walked into a recovery meeting hall and there she was. He could not believe it was her. He thought about her so often throughout the years. She was as strikingly beautiful as she had been twenty years earlier. It was 1989 and so much had changed. Sophie was divorced and lived in an apartment a few doors down from that particular meeting place. The apartment where she was living was in a building owned by a Collingdale judge and attorney, Ed Harkin.

The judge befriended Sophie or maybe Sophie befriended him. His wife was sick with cancer and he had a girlfriend and a reputation. He owned the building Sophie lived in and numerous other rental properties. He acted as the attorney for a Drexel Hill property owner. This woman was caught in a sting and charged with discrimination. She refused to rent to African Americans and/or people with children. The Fair Housing Council of Suburban Philadelphia wanted her to be forced to sell her properties and to pay some hefty fines.

The court ordered the woman to stop managing properties for five years. Harkin agreed to volunteer as her housing manager for one year. An organization that monitored housing complaints reported the woman never stopped managing her property. Harkin's failure to follow a court order was troubling, especially since he was an officer of the court.

Bob said shortly after he ran into Sophie again after all of those years, the judge sold the building that Sophie lived in and the new owners wanted her out. They wanted to open a pizza business downstairs and remodel the upstairs so they could live there themselves. Sophie dug her heels in and refused to move. The new owners had no other choice. They served her with eviction papers and when she still refused to budge, they hired men to break in to Sophie's apartment. They had every right to do so. It was their property. They had the men pack up Sophie's belongings and put them into a storage building. Bob was able to help her track down the men responsible and they charged Sophie a ridiculous amount of money for the information on where her belongings were being stored. Those thieves were paid by the judge and Sophie. Bob helped her recover her stuff from that storage unit and then he helped her move her belongings into storage.

At that time, Bob had recently moved his elderly mother in with him and his wife in Delaware and he asked Sophie if she would stay with and care for his mother while he and his wife went on vacation. Sophie was so relieved to be in a safe home. She was so exhausted. All she did for the first few days she was there was sleep. One day she put a pot of soup on the stove and fell sound asleep. Bob's mother who was not well smelled the pot burning and saved the house from burning down. She ended up taking care of Sophie for the rest of the week. Once Bob and his wife came home, Sophie wanted to be back in Delaware County.

I still had my doubts whether she actually was an alcoholic or for some reason being in the rooms of twelve-step programs gave her comfort. I wondered if her father was an alcoholic and brought her along with him to meetings when she was a child. She told me her husband was a mean alcoholic but never mentioned him going to any meetings or being in any kind of recovery program. I could be very wrong but I assumed he died an active alcoholic. I had no information to tell me he was dead. I just assumed he was. Bob confirmed for us that Sophie's husband was indeed an alcoholic. He too often wondered if she actually was a real alcoholic, on the border, or just wanted to belong to something, anything. He told me that even when he first met her all those years ago in the Wagon Wheel bar in Darby, she would have one or two drinks and sip them, making them last the entire night. She told me herself that was the way she always drank.

After more than twenty years in one twelve-step program or another, John pretty much knew all of the old-timers and most of them knew him. He wondered if it was possible that he knew Sophie's husband, sons, daughters, grandsons, brothers, or sisters. He continued to ask about Sophie subtly and to study faces, looking for one that might resemble Sophie. John continued to visit meeting places all over the county, the places he had not gone to in years or even forgot about, with hopes of running in to or finding some information on Sophie's relatives.

Sophie told me her daughter was in North Carolina so I figured it was mute to look for her. She told me her son Frankie was in California with an older woman and his small daughter. Her son Billy was our best bet. He was in the area, somewhere. I continued to try to find out what her maiden name was in the hopes of finding her siblings. She continued to be evasive. It was so frustrating. Why couldn't I make her understand I was trying desperately to reunite her with her own family? What was she afraid of? What was she hiding or who was she hiding from and why?

John was able to find out that there was an older man who took Sophie into his apartment and tried to help her. After a couple of months the man said he had no choice but to ask her to leave because she would not take care of herself. She refused to shower, do her laundry, or cook for herself. He was terminally ill and his family thought it was unhealthy for him to be living with the odor and the filth. They pressured him to throw her out. While I was angry with this man and his family at first for putting Sophie out into the street, I do understand. I was starting to realize Sophie was simply incapable of taking care of herself.

It was becoming obvious to John and me that we were not the first people to try to help Sophie. More and more she was reminding me of a little lost puppy that would find a good-hearted human being and stay with them until there were rules to follow. Rules that she did not want to follow or perhaps she was completely incapable of following for whatever reason. As soon as the gate was left open she would run off again. I was hoping at the least we would be able to break *that* cycle of taking off.

I was realizing more and more that this was not age-related dementia behavior. Was this a disability she was born with or was it something else related to her age?

In my work as a caregiver nearly all of the elderly clients I worked with disliked showers, baths, or anything that involved getting themselves wet. I wondered if it was all the literature and commercials with nurses and doctors warning about possible disastrous falls in the bathroom. It could be they do not like being cold. They are from the generation that grew up having one bath a week, usually on a Saturday night. Not one of my many clients ever gave me a direct answer as to why they hated to bathe. I decided to try some of the things I did for my clients with Sophie. I warmed her towels and her fresh clothes in the dryer. I placed a space heater in the bathroom. I made promises of hot soup, warm muffins, and hot chocolate as bribes. No matter what methods I used to get her into the bathroom it continued to be an all-day chore.

At least once a day, I did a Google search of Sophie's and her son's names. Nothing ever came up, not one word. She always changed the subject when I asked her what her maiden name was. It was so frustrating. They were out there somewhere, all of them. Why wasn't anyone missing and looking for her? Even more confusing to me was why didn't she want to be found?

Sophie with Santa Claus. Year unknown.

Sophie as a teenager.

The Stranger In My Recliner- Sophie 2010

Sophie- Year unknown.

Granddaughter -Adriana

Sophie's onetime apartment

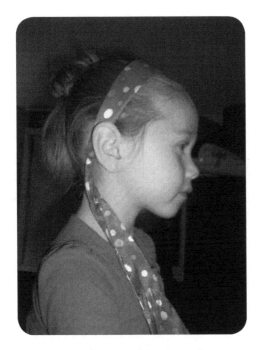

Avery Paige (tiny hiney)

Sophie's McDonalds (Chester Pike)

Doreen and her father, Frank - 2012

The property on MacDade Boulevard where
Sophie's father's business was located.

Doreen with grandsons Jimmy and Dominic.

Doreen and John McGettigan. We did it, Sophie, we got married in the church. Our Lady of Charity 2011.

Doreen and Michael 2011

Louie and Lance

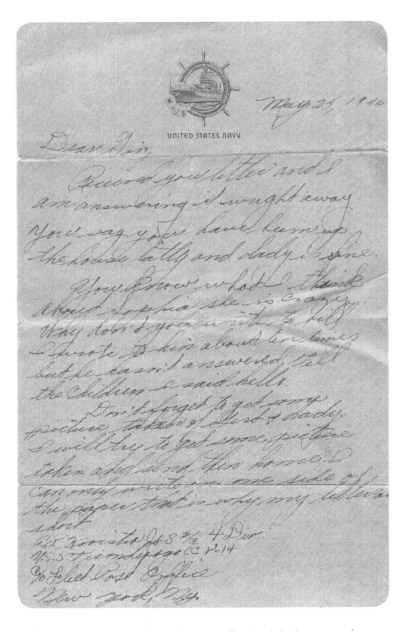

A letter from 1944 found among Sophie's belongings from
one of Sophie's relatives stating he thought she was crazy.
She kept it all those years. It must have really hurt her.

Sophie's McDonald's on Chester Pike

Granddaughters Avery and Morgan

Granddaughter Peyton Elizabeth and Louie.
Sophie and Louie were in love with her.

The property across from Sophie's father's business.
Sophie lived on this property as a child.

The sidewalk where John found Sophie "that night.

Sophie and Jim E. Curtin

Sophie and Jim E. Curtin, or is this Elvis?

Sophie (year unknown)

The view of Sophie's woods from Mac Dade
Boulevard. She slept on the other side of the hill.

Sophie's woods.

11

Gathering the Facts

We knew that while growing up, our Sophie lived on a hill in Ridley Township. That location is now the home to the Ridley Township Police Station and the Ridley Township Library. Across the street sitting catty-corner was a produce market. That market recently closed suddenly and will most likely become a bank. Sophie said when she was a little girl her father had a business at that location. He collected old radiators, heaters, copper tubing, and wiring, basically anything that he could repair and resell or scrap. Sophie told me story after story of the times she spent with her daddy there after her mother died.

When she told me the stories about her and her father, I could not help but picture in my mind a tall, handsome man with his beautiful blonde-headed little girl with the biggest and brightest blue eyes up on his shoulders, both of them smiling and laughing.

One day the two of them arrived at the shop to find it had been broken into and vandalized. Everything her father had in there of any value was stolen from the building. That was the end of his business. As she told me this story, I got the feeling

Sophie knew who it was that committed the burglary but she didn't tell me.

When she was a little girl, her brother kept a chicken in the basement. Just one chicken that laid one egg a day, sometimes two. Often when I made her scrambled eggs, she would tell me her brother was selfish and would never give her one of the chicken's eggs.

She said, "I was always nice to him and I really wanted to taste one of those eggs. He told me to catch my own chicken but I wasn't fast enough and he wouldn't help me."

I honestly did not know what to think of her family. I know it was a very long time ago, things were much different than they are now but a chicken running around in the basement? What kind of house was this? Was that a normal thing back then? Why didn't he build a little chicken coup in the backyard and add more chickens to it so the whole family could have fresh eggs for breakfast. It couldn't be very sanitary even in those days to have live poultry running around in the basement of one's house. Still the video in my mind of little girl Sophie running around trying to catch her own chicken made me smile.

She told me she was the youngest of six kids. Her father was married and had five kids. That wife either left or died and he then married Sophie's mother. Sophie said her mother died when she was very young. She told me her older brothers and sisters hated her because she was such a pretty little girl and her daddy loved her mother and her so much.

Much later, I found out she had a brother named Bill Kooster and a sister named Pauline Byer. Pauline might have been a half sister. Nobody I talked to seemed to know for sure. The more information I received on Sophie the more confused I became. She told me she was the only natural child between her mother and her father and now I was finding out about this full-blood brother, if it was true.

Bill Kooster lived in Newtown Square, Pennsylvania with his wife who was a Christian woman and their two daughters. Sophie was close with her sister-in-law, so her friend Bob would take her to visit her and Bill Kooster after his wife got sick. Her brother had no choice but to eventually move his wife into Fair Acres. Fair Acres is the state-run nursing home in our area. Bill could no longer care for his wife himself. Sophie wanted to move in and take care of her sister-in-law but Sophie said Bill's daughters were adamantly against the idea. When his wife passed away, Bill took it very hard and so did Sophie. She was angry with her brother for placing his beloved wife and her friend into Fair Acres.

Her brother Bill always tried to help Sophie and be there for her when she needed help. He would often visit her, leaving money sometimes two hundred dollars at a time.

Sophie hated twenty-dollar bills so as soon as her brother Bill gave her the money, she ran off to the store to exchange the twenties for tens. She was like that with us too. She always requested ten-dollar bills when I took her to the bank. She told me twenty-dollar bills were bad luck. When I asked her why she felt that way, she said she had no idea and she just knew it was so.

One of Sophie's brothers, I'm not sure of his name so I don't know if it was Bill Kooster or another brother, worked as a bass player for a country music star possibly Dolly Parton. Sophie owned all sorts of collectables from that brother. She never talked to me about this brother, his job or her collectibles. I wondered if all of these keepsakes he had given her were in one of her storage units. Was this how she came to own all of the Elvis memorabilia that I heard she had in her storage unit? Did she not tell me any stories about this brother because she knew I was a big country music fan and she was afraid I would steal her prized treasures? The thought of her not trusting me always hurt my feelings but I did understand why she might feel that way.

Sophie married very young and had two children, a son she named Billy and a daughter named Susan. They called Susan "Peaches." She told me her husband was abusive toward her and that the abuse started right from the moment they were married. She said at times he was abusive with her children too. He may have either lost one of his legs or badly injured his leg while deployed with the military. I found out that he had been a firefighter in Darby, Pennsylvania and he was a member of the Veterans of Foreign Wars.

Sophie repeated a story over and over to me about how her sister stole her husband from her and then stole her baby. This story was hard for me to listen to but I always did listen, hoping to gain just the tiniest shred of new information. Sometimes when she told me the story, she was so angry and other times, she would well up with tears. It was obvious that *something* happened and she was deeply hurt by her sister and her husband. What that truth was, I have no idea.

We know that her husband remarried and had at least four more children and he died in November of 2009, which is shortly after Sophie moved in with us. Did Sophie know he had died and if she did, how did she find out? Whenever she was out of the house it was always with us and she rarely talked to anyone when we were out. Why did she always tell me he died a long time ago? The only reason I could think of was she did not want me to find him. When I thought about it, I realized there was no way she could have known her ex-husband had died. We never left her alone long enough so it was nearly impossible for her to have known.

According to this obituary I found online, he lost his second wife before he passed and had other children, several more.

James C. Childs, Jr. 85 of Sharon Hill died Saturday November 7, 2009 at home.

Mr. Childs was a 1941 graduate of Eddystone High School, Served in the U.S. Navy 2nd Class Boatswain's Mate on *U.S.S. Massachusetts B.B. 59* He received a purple heart "Battle of Casablanca," Plank Owner of *U.S.S. Massachusetts.* Mr. Childs served as Staff Sgt. In the U.S. Marine Corps, He was a Life Member of the V.F.W. Post 7213 Norwood, PA. Life Member Disabled American Veterans & American Legion. Life Member and Past Officer of Colwyn Fire Co., Darby Fire Patrol #2 Darby Fire Co. #1 and Sharon Hill Fire Co.

Husband of the late Audrey A. Childs, and brother of the late Ralph Childs and Aileene Yeager.

Mr. Childs is survived by daughter Nancy Brown of Franklinville, NJ, son, William Childs of New Freedom, PA, Robert Childs of Cherry Hill, NJ, daughter Elizabeth Carry of Darby, PA, Susan Dreyer of Holmes, PA, Deborah Gallion of Willimgton, DE, Son, Scott Childs of Morton, PA. Caregivers Frank and Dana McBride, Grand-Dog's Zeus and Chuck, 16 Grandchildren, 11 Great-Grandchildren, and Nieces and Nephews.

The Funeral Service will be Celebrated 11 am on Wednesday at St. James Episcopal Church, 11th and Lincoln Ave., Prospect Park, PA. Visitation will be Tuesday evening 6–9pm at the Church and after 10am Wednesday. Burial is in Arlington Cemetery, Drexel Hill, PA.

When I read the line, survived by his grand-dogs Zeus and Chuck, all I could think was Oh my! The man was a disabled veteran and a firefighter so I couldn't help but think he had to have some redeeming qualities. I had many reasons to doubt Sophie's accounts of her life but I also had a gut feeling that a lot of what she told me was true. I wondered if she would have wanted to go to her ex-husband's funeral. I know I would have wanted to take her and be there for her. I couldn't help but feel I missed an opportunity to learn a lot more about her and her earlier years and her circumstances.

The most troubling story Sophie told me was that she was sexually assaulted and became pregnant. It was common knowledge in twelve-step circles that this "Al" person, the one who attacked Sophie, thought he was a big deal in recovery circles. He thought he was God's gift to beautiful young women. When Sophie rebuffed him, he pressured her, stalked her, and then he raped her. I am not certain if this happened while she was still married but I guessed it was long after she was divorced. She was in her forties when she had her second baby boy.

She insisted on keeping the baby, saying it wasn't the sweet little baby's fault. She named her baby boy Frankie and she adored him. Sophie told me that one day when her son was a few weeks old, her sister came to her house and told Sophie she was not feeding the baby correctly and she was going to take him away from her and find him a good home. Sophie was devastated. Sophie said she did everything she could possibly do to get him back but nobody was on her side.

She talked about that son each and every single day she was living with us. She said he was always a good boy, never any trouble and it was only when he hooked up with an older woman that was no good that he distanced himself from his mother.

"I blame her," Sophie kept telling me. "He loves me. I know he does. He only left me because of her."

I found out later that Sophie's sister, Pauline believed Sophie needed to be in a hospital for the mentally ill. Sophie's friend Bob believed that she was always slow but had no idea what sort of diagnosis she was ever given. I was starting to believe she was developmentally challenged and also had some sort of, or even several mental health disorders.

Her son Frankie did go to California when he was nineteen years old with a thirty-five-year-old woman. Sophie got herself onto a bus, headed to California, found him and was able to talk him into coming back home. Once back in Delaware County, Pennsylvania, Frankie had a daughter with another older woman. Sophie always told me he had the baby with *that* old lady but I found out it was with a different woman. Often, Sophie had Frankie and the little girl spend the night with her at her apartment.

I asked Sophie several times why she didn't call the police or try to get her infant son back and she told me she did try but nothing she did worked. Her sister continued to lie and tell the authorities that Sophie did not feed or care for the baby correctly. How could I help but wonder if her sister was right. The woman could not even operate a microwave or a TV remote control. How would she ever be capable of measuring formula? I found out later that Sophie's sister actually gave the baby to a couple and they moved to California with him. The facts were still so unclear to me. I still was unsure whether Sophie went to California at that time also to find her child when he was just a baby. What is clear is that she furiously fought city hall her entire life and never won.

I wondered why her sister didn't move Sophie and the baby in with her so she could keep an eye on them and help her out with the baby that she loved so much. If it was my sister, that's what I would have done. I would never rip a baby from the arms of a mother that loves him. I felt so bad for Sophie and for her son.

Sophie told her son, Frankie the circumstances surrounding his conception and birth. That must have been a hard thing to tell your kid and an even harder thing for a kid to hear. She told me Frankie thanked her for being honest with him. He also thanked her for being brave and for having him and for trying to take care of him on her own. If he felt that way about his mother where in the world was he? Was he not worried that she was living out in the cold, being robbed, or God forbid being assaulted again? What in the world happened to you that leaves you not knowing or caring where your mother is for months or even years?

I thought of the several kids I personally knew of that had no idea of how they came to be or who their real fathers were. Their mothers felt they were doing the best for these children by keeping their true heritage from them. Honestly, I could not disagree with a few of them and their reasons. One young woman I know was sexually assaulted when she fell asleep at a party. She became pregnant and made the decision to keep her baby. The rapist actually fought her furiously for visitation once she had the baby and the court granted it to him. The guy's family members, knowing what he did to this young girl, decided to support him in court. That poor young woman was put into a situation where she was repeatedly victimized physically and emotionally, not only by a rapist and his family but also by the system that is supposed to protect her. She found herself in a position where it was impossible for her to keep herself and her child safe. The system failed her and it was so infuriating and heartbreaking to watch. Thankfully our prayers were answered and that piece of trash was arrested for another crime and sent to prison for a very long time.

As much as I am able to understand why some horrible circumstances would keep these women from telling their child the truth about their heritage, I do also think it must make life sort of permanently off-balance for the mother and the child. Whatever Sophie's reason was for being honest with her son, I admired her for telling him the truth. It couldn't have been easy for her to admit to him or for him to hear but it was the right thing to do. I wondered if he ever confronted his father.

What I couldn't for the life of me understand was, if he thanked her for being brave and having him where the heck was he now? Where was his daughter? That little girl had to be a grown woman by the time Sophie was with us. She was at least a young adult by this time. Did she remember and miss Sophie? I was pretty sure Sophie missed her all the time. I had a feeling our granddaughter Avery reminded Sophie of this granddaughter.

Another story I heard was her daughter, Peaches got involved with Sophie's boyfriend. They decided they were going to go to North Carolina to find a house. They promised Sophie when they found a home they would come back for her and she could come to North Carolina to live with them. They never came back for her. I was able to find out that Peaches actually moved to Cape May, New Jersey not North Carolina. Did she tell Sophie she was moving to North Carolina and if she did, why? Sophie's son Billy built a duplex in Cape May, New Jersey and let Peaches and possibly Frankie live there. Since then Peaches built her own home in Cape May. Was this why Sophie wouldn't go to the shore with us? Was she afraid she might run into her kids on the beach? Maybe she thought we were planning on dumping her off with her son and daughter while we were there.

Sophie's friend Lisa told me that Peaches was always afraid her mother was going to steal her husband. I am not sure if this was Peaches's first husband or the second. She was married twice. I also didn't know if I should laugh or cry. Why would you marry someone that you were afraid would leave you for your mother? What an anxiety-filled and terribly sad way to live. This family did put *The Young and the Restless* story lines to shame.

I already told you the story about Billy's wife not getting along with Sophie. I found out that Billy was married to a woman named Vickie. They had two sons, Michael and Billy.

Billy and Vickie divorced. Vickie moved to Delaware, and Billy moved to Cape May, possibly with a woman named Bonnie. Sophie's friend Bob told me that Sophie always loved Billy's first wife Vickie. That sort of contradicted what Sophie said to me. She never ever mentioned Billy's sons to me, her own grandsons. I found that odd, especially if she liked and got along with their mother. Even odder was they had to be grown men. Where were they? Was Billy's longtime on-and-off girlfriend Bonnie the woman that she truly didn't get along with? Lisa told me that Sophie told her that Billy's sons did not care for Bonnie either.

We knew Sophie had a sister and a brother living in Newtown Square. Sophie loved her brother very much but his daughters were not fond of her and Sophie was not at all fond of them. She said they would make him kick her out of his house even if she was just there for a visit. What could she possibly have done to them? Where they jealous because their father loved his sister? Were they upset because he always gave her money? What did they know that I didn't know?

Sophie made it quite clear to me on many occasions she did not care for her sister one bit. I could not help but wonder if this was the sister who supposedly stole her husband and her baby Frankie. I knew she was the sister that tried to feed her chili after Sophie told her she did not like chili. Sophie told me this sister had all kinds of money but wasn't happy.

"She always want what me have and when I wouldn't give it to her, she stole it from me," she told me.

I found out later that Sophie believed Pauline would give her twenty-dollar bills to make herself look good in front of Sophie's friends and Sophie would put the money in her bag. When Sophie wasn't looking, Pauline would take the money back out of Sophie's bag. It was no wonder she was scared to put that ratty bag down anywhere. Whether the story was true or not, Sophie believed it was true. I wondered if it was possible she lost the twenty-dollar bills and only thought her sister took them back. Was this the reason she thought twenty-dollar bills were bad luck? It wasn't too absurd to think whatever "friend" brought Sophie to visit with her sister could have been a thief. Everyone wasn't as kind and caring with her as her friend Bob and her friend Lisa always were.

Sophie took an awful lot of pictures. She told me she was that Elvis impersonator's photographer. She loved disposable cameras and bought at least one almost every time I took her to a store. She had a collection of them. It was so odd though because she never had any of the photos developed. She would not let me take them to be developed. I was curious, more like obsessed to see the photos she took. I wanted to see a photo of that phony Elvis's so-called girlfriend. I still have a lot of those cameras. I am planning to have them developed.

Her friend Lisa told me that Sophie used to hang out at a Delaware County club called Sam's. She said Sophie had a knack for meeting, chatting with, and photographing famous people. At Sam's one night, she met Debbie Boone and had a long conversation with her. I wish I could have known that Sophie. Not that we didn't have many wonderful conversations because we did, I just always felt like she was holding back.

I found out that Sophie had been friends with Jim "E" Curtin's mother for years. Curtin would take Sophie and his new girlfriend into restaurants and he would order all kinds of food and then he would pick a fight with the servers and refuse to pay the check. Original idea he had, right? Sophie and this girlfriend fought like cats and dogs. This girlfriend of his did go after Sophie in the storage unit. The woman that worked at the facility called the police and they ended up taking Sophie to the hospital where they put her on the psych floor and held her for twenty-four hours. The police must get frustrated trying to defuse situations but dear Lord, Sophie was injured. Why wasn't the girlfriend arrested? Did Sophie refuse to press charges against her because she didn't want Curtin to be upset with her?

Sophie was also friendly with Curtin's son and he actually lived in the apartment below Sophie in Collingdale. The same building that Judge Harkin owned, eventually sold and the new owners had her evicted because they wanted to open a pizza shop in the building. I recently found out when the new owner was renovating that apartment, he found one of Sophie's social security checks under the carpet. Years before that check was discovered under that carpet, she accused everyone she knew of stealing it out of her bag.

She was apparently always very forgetful. Her friend Bob told me that Sophie got around riding busses for years. That was something she never told me. Back then she would often forget her pocketbook, leaving it behind on the bus seat. The driver's knew her well and would hold the bag for her. In the meantime Sophie would accuse everyone she knew of stealing the bag.

Hearing this information once again filled me with doubt and caused me to rethink everything Sophie ever told me. How much was actually taken from her in her life and how much had she herself just forgotten or misplaced. It was sad that I was starting to be able to picture her misplacing the missing money, items, or even perhaps her own baby.

Was it possible she was leaving our house and riding the bus to visit her own family members and friends? Maybe she had contacted them and let them know she was safe and being cared for in our home. Honestly the thought made me feel like an idiot because I never considered it before. There was a bus stop right at the top of our street. Where I grew up, there were no busses, so they were not a mode of transportation that automatically came to mind for me.

I needed to open my mind a bit more when it came to Sophie's children and her siblings. Everyone has a story and I didn't know what their side of this story was. Some of the pieces were starting to come together but there was still so much we did not know about this stranger in our recliner.

Criminalizing Homelessness and the Mentally Ill

Unfortunately, some people think the best way to handle the homeless epidemic is to criminalize the homeless. It is horrifying to think the people with these ideas are leaders, and these are the best solutions they could come up with.

Hawaii state representative Tom Bower would smash the shopping carts of homeless people if he found them sleeping during the day.

Columbia South Carolina gave the homeless the option to relocate or be arrested. They rescinded after backlash from police and advocates.

An ordinance Tampa, Florida, making it illegal to sleep or store personal property in public. They followed the law up with another law, this one against panhandling.

Philadelphia banned the feeding of the homeless on city parkland. Religious groups refused to obey the law. John and I ignore this rule as well. We will continue to hand out sandwiches.

Authorities from Raleigh, North Carolina, asked religious groups to stop feeding the homeless in a downtown park on the weekends.

I think the state of Utah has a much better idea. Do you remember Gov. John Huntsman? He ran for president. I believe this was his idea and it is brilliant!

In 2005, Utah realized it was cheaper to provide the homeless with an apartment and a social worker than it was to keep sending them to the local emergency rooms and to jail. The program is called "Homes Not Handcuffs," and over the years, the program has reduced the homeless population in Utah by 78 percent. I would call that a success.

I am not a fan of giving money and moving on. If that is truly all you can possibly do, then yes money does help but money and "doing" are so much better. When we give someone that hand up shouldn't we do all we can to also help them stay up? How does that saying go give someone a fish and they will eat dinner tonight but if you give them a fishing rod and teach them to fish, they can eat every night. The state of Utah went the extra mile by providing not only an apartment but a social worker that teaches them, the once homeless, how to keep that new apartment and more.

There is a growing poverty rate in America. The Department of Housing and Urban Development shows five million Americans are at risk of becoming homeless every year.

The government keeps building shelters and then they mismanage them so that they are nothing more than magnets for criminals. They are by design almost always in the worst parts of a city on purpose, to keep the crime in the high crime area. Only now, it isn't just criminals that are homeless. It is veterans, young adults, mothers with children, and even families with children, pets and the elderly.

In most cities in the United States the property and occupational taxes have been raised so high that only the wealthiest people can afford to live there. The poorest people and those that are homeless choose to live on the streets in cities because they are closest to train stations, bus terminals and libraries, places they can gather to keep warm and blend in with the crowds. They can become invisible. Inner city police are unlikely to respond and even less likely to take any action against the homeless or mentally ill because they are too few and too busy with homicides, assaults and other violent crimes. Other urban poor people live in public housing or subsidized housing. The middle class have all but disappeared from our inner cities and sadly, they are rapidly disappearing from the suburbs as well.

There are so many abandoned or foreclosed bank-owned homes. Instead of building shelters, wouldn't it be great if mortgage companies started a special program that took applications from homeless families and moved them into these homes? They could move them into the property on the condition that they work with a financial expert, provided by the bank that could help the family become financially fit within a determined amount of time. Once that was done, the family could buy the home from the bank. I am not a financial expert by any means but wouldn't a program like that benefit the banks greatly in the long run?

A number of public libraries across the country have hired social workers because of the overwhelming numbers of homeless people using their buildings to stay warm in the winter and cool in the summer. These people are also using library bathrooms to sleep, to bathe in, and to wash their clothes.

Again, this reminds me of the question, why do the rights of one homeless person who has not had a shower in weeks and is filthy, smelly, and possibly mentally ill trump the rights of the twenty-five other people in the library? A student working on a term paper, a writer doing research, a woman recently diagnosed with cancer using the computer to see what options are available to her, and a young mother with two or three young children who are choosing DVDs. Does that mother not have a right to bring her children into a public building with the reasonable assumption that they won't get scabies or lice?

I know 99.9 percent of people diagnosed with mental health disorders would never intentionally hurt anyone but what if that .01 percent was in that library and attacked that innocent student on that particular day? This weighs heavy on my mind. I feel morally compelled to help that homeless person, but I also want to assume that library is doing everything in their power to insure my visit to their building with my grandchildren is a safe and happy one.

I do believe homeless people have rights and no one should take those rights away from them. It gets so complicated and confusing because I don't want to give up my rights for their rights. People with a diagnosed mental illness have rights too, and to me that makes no sense whatsoever. I have *no* idea what the solution would be, but I definitely believe the mentally ill should not be making decisions about their mental health care. They should absolutely have advocates, or professionals to do that for them. I realize this is so much easier said than done. Not all professional are good and many do not even agree on diagnoses. Not all family members have the mentally ill person's best interest in mind. Even more, family members have simply become too frustrated to deal with a loved one that refuses to take meds and follow simple rules.

Should we resort to forcing these people to take medication that makes them lethargic, fat and sick to their stomachs but keeps them from having frightening outbursts? Definitely more work has to be done when it comes to researching the correct cocktail of medications for someone who has been diagnosed with a disorder. More attention has to be paid to the adverse side effects of all psychiatric drugs because, dear Lord, it is hard enough to manage a mental illness without taking a medication that causes high blood sugar and requires the mentally ill person to need to know and remember how to monitor sugars and use insulin.

I cannot get away from the idea that if we were able to manage our mentally ill loved ones in our homes, the numbers of the mentally ill homeless would go down drastically. If we could only be permitted to make the sometimes life-improving decisions without our hands being tied with the never-ending red tape that prevents rational decisions being made based on the personal knowledge we have of our loved ones. I imagine how life changing it could be for all involved if the help of several reliable lifelines were made available to caregivers, as well as advocates put in place to assist when a crisis does occur.

Would this be expensive to put together? Absolutely, it will be expensive but imagine the savings to taxpayers in the long run and more importantly imagine how the quality of life would change for the mentally ill and their caregivers. Our communities, first responders, and medical facilities would benefit financially as well.

12

The Feebleminded

Not that long ago, as a society, we locked away our family members that were deemed mentally ill or developmentally challenged. We locked them far away from the rest of us and our civilized society. We put them in dark cold asylums. In the 1500s, prior to having actual asylums to commit them to, they were put on asylum ships. Back then, these were known as the ships of fools. These ships roamed the seas and stopped from port to port, only to pick up supplies and more fools. Can you imagine who the people were that they hired to work on those ships? I am quite sure they were plucked from the crop of the least employable. Some of the workers were lifelong criminals. They were given the chance to be sentenced to the prison ship or to work on the ship of fools. Why not get rid of two of society's ills on one ship?

Some families, although very few back then, kept their feebleminded relatives locked away in the attics or the basements of their own homes for their entire lifetimes to protect them and to keep them safe from the horrors of those ships and asylums.

During the 1600s and 1700s, the practice of exiling our mentally ill from ordinary society continued. The purpose of this treatment was to remove and isolate the less desirable from society, rather than to try curing them or at least trying to help them with their symptoms. It wasn't until the early 1900s that a more compassionate attitude toward the mentally ill started to emerge but isolation was still the "normal" treatment.

Back then they were called the feebleminded. What does *feebleminded* mean anyway? I always wondered. The term was first used in the year 1534. Prior to 1534 the mentally ill or developmentally challenged were referred to as fools or idiots. The word *feebleminded* describes someone who was foolish or stupid, a person who makes less than sensible decisions routinely. That could be said of most of our politicians or any one of us at certain times of our lives. For most of us, I think we do something foolish at the least once a day.

Prior to the insane being cast out on to the ships of fools, it was left up to the family to care for them. If they were unable to manage the care of their loved one, the clergy and the community assisted. Back then, insanity was considered to be demonic or supernatural. It was not considered a health or medical condition.

The common practices in most of those asylums or "crazy houses" as they were called back then subjected our mentally challenged folks to horrific experiments and inhumane treatment. Just think *One Flew Over the Cuckoo's Nest* or *Girl, Interrupted.* Both very eye-opening cinematic accounts of practices that most likely in real life were far worse than what was portrayed on the big screen.

As a country, we came together and corrected these atrocities, or so we thought. We were fooled into believing that our government actually cared about our mentally ill citizens. Politicians gave flowery heartwarming speeches declaring our "crazy" friends and relatives have the same rights that we all have. They have the right to not to be locked away in institutions, attics, or basements. They deserve not to be tortured and used as guinea pigs throughout their entire lifetimes for the sake of science. Research animals were treated to better living conditions than our mentally ill. We were told that they all deserved to be not only living in communities with the rest of us but also contributing to our communities. They deserved to experience the love of their family and friends. They deserved to feel joy and to be happy. Who could argue with any of that?

The truth is that what our government cared about back then was all about redirecting money from a system that was about to crash and burn. Also headed for the ashes with the institutions were the many crooked politicians, shady large-business owners, and state and federal officials that for centuries had been greasing each other's palms and scratching each other's backs.

Stop and think for a minute about all of those asylums. Almost every city in America had at least one. Most of them were run by the city, state, and federal governments. They had to be expensive to maintain and of course, there were the never-ending lawsuits that were threatening impending doom for all who were intertwined in the networks of chronic wrongdoing in those facilities.

I wondered if Sophie's family ever talked about putting her into an institution. Did she grow up hearing those frightening conversations between the adults she loved and trusted? Did she grow up fearing she would be sent away from her home, her family, and everything and everyone familiar to her? I now know that her sister thought she needed to be in a mental institution. Did the sister feel that way for Sophie's entire lifetime because she was a feebleminded child? Maybe when her father passed away, she had nobody left in her corner to protect and look after her. Did her siblings want to be rid of the responsibility of her? Could that be the reason she did not trust her sisters and brothers? Were they relieved when she married a man even though he did not have her best interest at heart? Did they know she was being mistreated and look the other way?

Perhaps they all did try to take care of her. Maybe she was so strong-willed and stubborn that she refused to listen to them. That scenario was not that hard to imagine. Sophie definitely could be one tough woman when she wanted to be. If she didn't want to do it, there wasn't much chance of convincing her to do it. Was I starting to empathize with Sophie's family? I might have been at least trying to put myself in their shoes but no matter how I tried to walk in those shoes, it always led me to the conclusion that they gave up, washed their hands of a woman that no matter how strong-willed she was, she was incapable of taking care of herself and that made all of them responsible for all of the bad things that happened to her. If they couldn't come together and get along as a family in order to come up with a plan to keep Sophie safe, then shame on them.

Did they do any research on whatever Sophie's condition was? I know her son Billy did make the effort to place her in several different nursing home-type facilities but Sophie simply walked out. Did that give him the right to throw his arms up in the air and rid himself of the responsibility of his feebleminded mother? Did the rest of their family support his decisions or fight him on them?

Matthew Quick's book and subsequent movie adaption by David O'Russell *Silver Linings Playbook* provided more of a current-day look at the realities of mental illness and the effect it can have on families and entire communities. What I loved about that story was the way that Matthew created the "feebleminded" characters to be loveable and human without sugarcoating the fact that the possibility of dangerous and violent behavior was always there. He used comedy to inform us, and that softened the blow of the harsh reality that all of the medications and treatments available to those suffering with mental disorders are still pathetically cruel. There are so many new medications available now with more being created every day, yet they all still have long laundry lists of life-altering negative side effects. The side effects are sometimes worse than the effects of the mental illness.

In his book, Matthew also effectively portrayed how mental illness often "runs" in families and how family members with mental health disorders themselves are often the only caregivers available for other family members with mental health disorders.

Were there other members of Sophie's immediate family with some sort of disorder or developmental challenge too? Could that explain the dysfunction and complete breakdown of her family?

In his 1986 novel *Forrest Gump*, author Winston Groom's title character is written as an *idiot savant*. Savant syndrome is a condition where the afflicted can test extremely low on a standard IQ test, yet they can have exceptional, even sometimes considered to be brilliant, skills in math, art, music, and memory. Savant syndrome is caused by damage to the left anterior temporal lobe. This is the area of the brain that processes sensory input.

There is no agreement on how many people may have savant skills. The estimates range from extremely rare to one in ten of those diagnosed with autism having skills that would be considered unusual for "normal" people. It is not even considered a medical condition or a mental health condition.

Of course, the name *idiot savant* along with Forrest's sexual escapades never made it into the subsequent Academy Award–winning movie adaption of the novel.

I wasn't noticing any exceptional math or art skills in Sophie, and I was always looking for them. What I did notice was her cunning, shrewdness, and her street smarts—skills that she needed to survive out there on the streets. These were smarts that she needed to protect herself out there from the people that were mentally ill and violent. She also needed to watch out for the drug- and/or alcohol-addicted thieves and the chronically impoverished. Her street smarts would surely put any urban dweller to shame.

I continued to be curious and to ask Sophie about her mother. Like she always did, she'd simply say she died. The fact that Sophie did not get along well with women troubled me. She did not care for her own mother, her sisters, or her very own daughter. She didn't care much for me either, but I was passionate about and determined to get her to give me a chance, reasons to trust me. I constantly reminded her that I did not believe in any type of girl-on-girl meanness. I often told her that I believed that as women, we needed to focus on what we all had in common and to be there for each other, to support each other on what we have in common and to agree to disagree on our differences. Whenever I brought up this particular conversation, she would look at me like I was the one that was out of my mind. Maybe I was being idealistic in believing that it was possible for all of us women to at least have each other's back whether we agreed with one another or not. I did know firsthand what it was like to have a mother that hurt me deeply.—A mother that I was able to forgive and still be smart enough to get the fact that she would never have my best interests at heart and I could never again trust that she would.

Sophie did seem to like little girls. She spoke lovingly of her youngest granddaughter, her son Frankie's little girl. She had no time for our older granddaughters, and she even went as far as to enjoy agitating them. Being teenagers, they gave it right back to her. We spoke with them and explained to them that Sophie may need a little extra understanding, and we asked them to be patient with her and kind no matter what she said or did to them. They made us proud and poured on the love. They were able to wear Sophie's guard down and every now and then, we did see Sophie crack a smile their way.

She adored our youngest granddaughters. Was it their innocence she was attracted to and loved about them? Was there someone who stole her innocence away from her? Someone who stole her happy childhood from her? Sadly, I knew what that was like too and I told Sophie some stories from my own childhood. I hoped my story of being sexually assaulted by a trusted adult would help her open up to me some more about her own childhood. Every now and then she gave me a glimpse, but those moments were few and far between.

One day for the heck of it, I asked her if there were other people living back there in the woods were she had stayed. As soon as I asked her that question, I was sorry I asked. I did not want to know the answer. She told me there were quite a few other people living back there. Most of them were drug addicts.

"They be the ones that beat me up and steal from me," she said, putting her head down as if she was ashamed. Why in the world did I ask? She went on to tell me there was a sad old man living in those woods. He was sick, and he had no one who loved him or wanted to take care of him. She told me she used to try to take care of him by bringing him cheeseburgers from McDonald's and water that he used for drinking and washing. She also brought him aspirin because he was always in a lot of pain. Sophie definitely had a caregiver's heart to go with her shrewd street smarts.

That story was exactly the one I did not want to hear. I cried for a man I did not know. For a fleeting minute, I wondered if I should take Sophie with me and go into those woods to find that man. It was a ridiculous idea, but I couldn't stop thinking about him and hoping he was okay. It was impossible for me to get help for the one homeless person already living in my house. The thought of something that happened to my daughter popped into my mind. When she was eight months pregnant and working at a Sunrise assisted living home, she had been trying to help an elderly resident, a man to take a shower. He punched her in the face and because she was not expecting it, she lost her balance and fell backward onto the floor. Thank God, my daughter only got a black eye and minor injuries. My unborn granddaughter was fine. I don't believe that man wanted to hurt my daughter and her baby, but he wasn't capable of thinking correctly. Those memories were enough to get me to squash the idea of going anywhere near those woods looking to bring an elderly homeless man home with me. I still felt guilty and had trouble getting that poor old guy and his predicament out of my thoughts. I prayed that someone else found him and helped him so at least he was able to die with a shred of dignity and not at the hands of some thugs in those woods.

I thanked God that I always had a roof over my head. I prayed that my family would never hate me so much or that I never hurt anyone so severely that it would cause them to hate me that intensely that I would be sentenced to sleeping in the dark cold woods alone. I am terrified to go camping and sleep in a tent. I am also terrified of the dark and I get cold very easily. I would never be able to survive out there on my own.

As a child, I developed a fear of any type of forest or even the simplest patch of trees. My fear was the result of a frightening episode in the woods when I was ten years old. All this talk with Sophie about those other homeless people living in the woods had me thinking about that frightening episode from all those years ago. It had been so long since I thought about it and now I couldn't seem to shake that and a few other frightening memories from my childhood.

The novel *One Flew Over the Cuckoo's Nest* was written by Ken Kesey in 1959 and published in 1962. The novel was surely created from the author's real-life experience as a volunteer for several government projects. Those projects involved doing research on human beings, hoping to discover the benefits of the use of LSD, mescaline, and other psychoactive drugs on the mind. At the same time, Kesey worked the graveyard shift as an orderly at a mental health institution in California. There he had the opportunity to speak at great length with the patients and was also able to study the inner workings of the hospital. The author also openly admitted to using psychoactive drugs recreationally. He believed drug use was a path to individual freedom. Kesey said his use of the drugs made him deeply sympathetic of the patients in the institution.

I was tricked into taking mescaline. It was put into my ice tea when I was only fifteen years old. That was one of the most frightening experiences of my life. There were no beautiful vivid colors, no profound messages, and definitely no cute, fuzzy, talking animals. There was nothing but monsters and screaming black clouds. I cannot even imagine how terrifying it would be to have my brain stuck in that terrifying place indefinitely. A bad drug trip like the one I had is the way I always imagined mental illness to be. I swore if I lived through that experience, I would never do anything like that to my brain and I haven't.

My father told me drugs were around during the fifties, and he was just a bit younger than Sophie. He grew up in the same area. I asked her if she ever smoked pot or took any more serious drugs.

"No, me only drink alcohol and when me drink I sip one drink or two all night."

She told me several stories of how she tried and was sometimes able to help people that had terrible drug problems.

"They can't help themselves. They so sick."

One Flew Over the Cuckoo's Nest depicts the lives of several institutionalized, insane characters, and the staunch nurse charged with keeping them in line. The novel was published at the same time the controversial move toward closing the nation's government-run mental health facilities was taking place. It was also the same time in history that our country was either fighting for/or against civil rights. Sophie was in her late teens and living in the suburbs of Philadelphia, which at that time was the most "it" place in the country to be if you were a fan of pop or rock music.

During the late fifties and early sixties, the city of Philadelphia was the center of the pop music scene. It was still a few years before the British invasion and local musicians like Charlie Gracie, Chubby Checker, Bobby Rydell, and the Dovells along with record labels, recording studios, and distribution companies were enjoying great success. Sophie was a huge fan of the Philadelphia sound, but she was in love with the King of Rock and Roll, Elvis.

Sophie told me she was a fan of *American Bandstand* long before Dick Clark took over the show and then took it national in the late 1950s. The original host, Bob Horn was convicted of drunk driving and accused with, but acquitted of statutory rape charges.

Sophie held a grudge against Dick Clark for taking the *Bandstand* show to California. It is possible that the ambitious Dick Clark held a grudge against the city of Philadelphia for bringing charges of having a conflict of interest against him because he had financial interests in a few of the record companies in town.

Sophie didn't care much for the Beatles either. She was convinced they stole the spotlight from Elvis and her beloved Philadelphia singers.

Sophie was a gorgeous teenager with bouncy long blonde hair and piercing blue eyes. She knew an awful lot about the music scene in Philadelphia. I wondered how much she knew about the controversial changes that were simultaneously happening in the mental health industry, not only in the Philadelphia area but also across the country. I guessed she didn't know much, and if she did, she didn't care. Like most teenagers of her generation, she was interested in music and dancing and finding a way to get in to see Elvis up close and personal.

She continued to love and support her favorite musicians from the Philadelphia tri-state area. She loved it when I picked up magazines for her with articles about Bruce Springsteen or put in one of his CDs while we were in the car. Taylor Swift was a tough sell with Sophie being she was a female artist. I did my best to convince her that Taylor was a talented, innocent young girl, so she agreed to listen to her.

She was a huge Teddy Pendergrass fan and told me she always felt sorry for him because his mother was murdered when he was only twelve years old. Teddy started his musical career in Philadelphia as a drummer. He was asked to join Harold Melvin & the Blue Notes as their drummer but was quickly promoted to be the group's lead singer position. In the late seventies, he left the group and launched a successful solo career. In 1982, he was in an auto accident that resulted in him being paralyzed from the chest down. Sophie was convinced that he drank and had a hard time being happy because of the tragic loss of his mother. She was so sad when he died at the young age of fifty-nine.

In his novel *One Flew Over the Cuckoo's Nest*, which he titled after a nursery rhyme, Kesey writes one of his main characters, the Chief, as the narrator. He refers to many different authorities controlling individuals through coercion throughout the book. Like the *Forrest Gump* movie, many racier parts of the *Cuckoo's Nest* novel were edited out for the film that was released nearly twenty years later in 1975. That movie went on to win five Academy Awards. In the movie adaption, the Chief is a quiet background character that is brought to the forefront several times throughout and at the end of the movie when he finally breaks out of the institution.

One Flew Over the Cuckoo's Nest continues to be one of America's most highly challenged and banned novels. The book is still considered to be extremely pornographic, one that glorifies criminal activity, and would be likely to corrupt teenagers. It is also filled with bizarre violence and descriptions of beastiality.

John and I watched that movie with Sophie one night and all she ever said to us about the movie was that she hated the ending. That wasn't saying much because Sophie hated the ending of almost all of the movies we watched with her. In fact, the only movie we ever watched with her that she liked the ending to was the *Notebook*.

She always laughed when we were watching a baseball game and John yelled out, "Somebody get me a weiner," whenever our team was doing well. I wanted to ask her so badly if she was ever in an institution like that, but something told me that was not a good idea.

Things have changed drastically for those with mental health disorders, syndromes, and intellectual or physical disabilities. For the most part, the children with these conditions are now living in and being taken care of in their homes by their parents. Some families have in-home caregivers, physical therapists, and nurses. They also depend heavily on support from community health and mental health centers or clinics. Most of these families struggle to find in-home care so they can go to work. The system is set up that in order for families to qualify for assistance with medical bills and in-home care, you must be low income. If you work outside of the house and earn a decent salary, the cost for in-home or respite care is astronomical. Many mothers of special needs children give up on their out-of-the-house careers and opt to become their child's primary caregiver because they have no other choice.

Once a child that has a mental health disorder or an intellectual disability grows up and becomes an adult, his or her parents' hands can quickly become tied when it comes to making decisions for their grown child's care. I know enough people that have been in this position to know how frustrating the "system" can be. Suddenly their child is considered an adult legally and looks like an adult physically but is still very much a child mentally and emotionally. These children suddenly have the right to make their own choices when it comes to their care, and that can have devastating repercussions for them, their families, and sometimes their communities.

I wish we would go back to treating all of our mentally ill and developmentally challenged patients in our communities the way we did prior to the 1500s but knowing what we know now. Back then, religious organizations and neighbors were great financial and emotional support systems for families that were caring for the insane or for children that were intellectually challenged.

It has been a long time since the term *feebleminded* was used. We have definitely not come a long way. *Feebleminded* was replaced by other terms like *deranged, lunatic, maniac, nut, psychopath, idiot, imbecile, retarded, loony, cuckoo, mad,* and so many more. While it is not considered politically correct to use any of these words to describe the mentally ill or developmentally challenged, they are all still used. We should all worry less about the names being used and start worrying more about the lack of effective medication, treatment options, and care.

13

Byberry

Known as the father of modern psychiatric medicine, Benjamin Rush, one of the signers of the Declaration of Independence, believed that mental diseases were caused by irritation of the blood vessels in the brain. In the 1700s, he treated patients by bleeding them, immersing them in very hot or very cold water, or giving them mercury. He invented a tranquilizer chair intended to calm patients. What the chair did was confine them until they calmed down. In that sense, I guess it worked. He published many papers and gave lectures.

Benjamin Franklin, another founding father, strongly believed those citizens who were sick in their minds should be subsidized comfortably by the government.

One of the places intended to house those mentally afflicted citizens comfortably was the Philadelphia Hospital for the Mentally Ill. It was founded in the 1700s within the city limits. It was later moved to the farthest northeast section of the city and became known as Byberry Hospital. Founded under the best intentions but with a serious lack of funding, oversight, and qualified help doomed the institution from the start. Rumors of abuse, assault, neglect, and even murder ran rampant through the community, city, and state. The asylum was run by corrupt city politicians from day one. Patients were left shackled for years, urinated all over themselves, and were left to sit on cold wet floors, naked.

In 1907, an employee strangled a patient until that patient's eyes popped out of their sockets. That employee was fired. He was not arrested and charged with murder. There was no long-drawn-out investigation of the policies and procedures or the lack of training of the staff. The employee was simply fired. Once the attention died down, that employee was quietly reinstated. There are many rumors that this was not the only horrific murder at Byberry. The shell game practice of moving troubled politicians, officials, or employees still happens today. Not much has changed politically speaking.

Political discord and rhetoric are nothing new in this country. We should all stop pretending that it is something so *hateful* and so *different* now from anything it ever was in the past. Politics today is the same nasty business it always was. The only difference nowadays is the job pays much better.

As early as 1911 and repeatedly through the years, journalists from the *Philadelphia Inquirer*, the *Philadelphia Daily News*, *Time* magazine, the *Tribune Business*, the *New York Star*, and many more investigated, reported on, and shamed the state of Pennsylvania because of its lack of corrective action at the state hospital. Several books were written about the hospital too. Steps would quickly be taken by the management to correct the atrocities while the spotlight was shining on them. As soon as the attention from the media stopped, the employees reverted back to the same old deplorable behavior.

The abuse was so blatant that in 1936, a grand jury was convened. In 1938, that grand jury insisted the state immediately take over the managing of the facility. The transfer did little to nothing to change the conditions. The staff, management, politicians, and officials spent all of their time fighting with one another so nothing actually changed. At that time, the institution was warehousing six thousand patients. They were lucky if they received basic custodial care.

One of the most horrid stories I heard was of a doctor who was studying child molesters. He took children that were wards of the state, perhaps because they had syndromes or were orphans, or for any number of other reasons. This doctor placed those children in rooms with the most horrific child molesters and watched as the children were physically, mentally, and sexually assaulted. He did this in the name of medical research. I cried when I first heard that story, and it still affects me today. We know there were no cures or great treatments to come out of that doctor's research. The most innocent and helpless little children endured lives of torture and probably died alone.

I cannot help but wonder what I would have done if I worked there or had a loved one in that house of horrors. All I had to do was look at the blue recliner in my living room to know the answer to that question. If I lived back then and worked in that dungeon, my first instinct would most likely have been to open the doors and let everyone out of that godforsaken place. Then I most likely would have realized that simple gesture, although with the best of intentions in mind, would not work without a well-drafted plan. A plan that included some sort of community education and a far and wide safety net put in place to protect both the patients and the community.

Strangely, the first people to publically come out and demand better treatment for the people kept in Byberry were the conscientious objectors to World War II. These people were given the opportunity to work in the wards of state hospitals all over the country to fill the void left by the regular staff members that went into the military. They were the first to alert the government about the mistreatment of patients and the blatant misappropriations of funds. They said the treatment was worse than the treatment given our soldiers by the Nazis in their war camps. The government not being able to ignore the reports any longer because of the sheer number of these whistle-blowers cancelled the military contracts that they had with these facilities to care for our soldiers that were suffering from shell shock.

Thank goodness, finally, those poor people were going to get some help, and they would finally receive at least the most basic of human care. Then I think about that for a minute. The government, our elected politicians, cancelled contracts with its own government-run facilities and then did nothing to correct the problems in any of those facilities. They simply shut the whistle-blowers up, which made the media go away, and the same bad behavior by employees restarted right where it left off.

Although the horrors were many and dominate most written recollections of these institutions, most of them across the country were full of unsung heroes. There were nurses and attendants that demonstrated compassion for the residents. There are many stories left untold of kind staff members taking the residents on picnics and walks around the grounds on warm, sunny days. They used their own money to buy toys and clothing for the feebleminded children and were there to offer hugs and to tuck them in at night.

Some of the country's best psychiatric doctors struggled with and worked endless hours in these facilities trying to come up with better treatments, medications, and cures for mental illnesses.

During the 1940s, the census at Byberry grew to over seven thousand patients.

The 1950s brought with it many changes to treatment and promising new medications. Those medications such as Thorazine allowed some patients to function almost normally. Unfortunately, the side effects of Thorazine were not known until years later.

Tardive dyskinesia was just one condition that began to appear in many patients that had been treated with Thorazine and some other antipsychotic medications. The simple definition of tardive dyskinesia is involuntary movements. These movements sometimes didn't start until the medication was discontinued. It happened in patients that were treated long term with the drug, as well as in those that were only taking it for only a brief time. The involuntary movements affected the tongue, jaws, and mouth and caused such things as rhythmical chewing. Another side affect that occurred was shuffled walking or the dragging of one foot. How many horror movie images does that bring up? There are a number of other irreversible conditions that occurred, including epilepsy due to side effects from the use of these antipsychotic drugs. Some of them are still in use today, and the decision to prescribe them stems from weighing the seriousness of the patient's symptoms versus the side effects.

Reading about the rhythmic chewing side affect was fascinating to me because I work with elderly clients, and I have known a few that had that uncontrollable chewing condition. I couldn't help but wonder what medications they had been on when they were younger and why. Did they even realize what caused them to have the condition and that it was a side effect from medication they may have taken years before?

As John F. Kennedy began his administration in the 1960s, intellectual disabilities and mental health disorder research was basically ignored and neglected by scientist and doctors. Few caregivers were trained in effective, responsible care of these patients. With the urging of his sister Eunice, President Kennedy brought these disabilities out of the shadows and into the public light. With the Kennedys, it was personal. The president's younger sister Rosemary was intellectually disabled. Before he was even inaugurated, he created a task force. Once he was in office, he followed the task force's recommendation to establish the National Institute of Child Health and Human Development. The institute is still in existence today and supports research on developmental disorders.

Nine months after the inauguration, at a press conference on October 11, 1961, President Kennedy announced his intention to appoint "a panel of outstanding scientists, doctors, and others to prescribe a plan of action in the field of mental retardation." He added, "The central problems of cause and prevention remain unsolved, and I believe that we as a country, in association with scientists all over the world, should make a comprehensive attack." The twenty-seven-member panel met with President Kennedy at the White House on October 18, 1961.

On October 24, 1963, President Kennedy signed the Maternal and Child Health and Mental Retardation Planning Amendment to the Social Security Act, the first major legislation to combat mental illness and retardation.

President John Kennedy also announced in 1963 that he believed and felt strongly that the mentally ill should be taken care of in their homes with assistance from the government and the community. He was motivated by the mental illness of his own sister. Critics would say it was more likely the matter of hundreds of looming lawsuit judgments due to abuse, neglect, rape and murder and a lack of federal funds to pay them that motivated him.

He wanted to begin by involving communities in the happenings at the asylums. He wanted church groups and young children to visit to humanize the patients. Photo opportunities that provided the scenes in black and white that would be used to in a roundabout way to brainwash us. We would be called to action and have to do something to help these human beings.

Community mental health centers started to pop up in communities across the country. Valium and other mental health drugs were prescribed like aspirin in record numbers. Homemakers and mothers across the country were better able to cope with a world that was changing rapidly. The awful side effects of these drugs were also still unknown at that time.

I witnessed my own mother carried out of our house on a stretcher after taking valium and then drinking Harvey's Bristol Cream in the 1960s. I was six years old. I thought she was dead. She was home the next morning and nothing more was ever said about the incident. It frightened me so much that it instilled in me a lifelong fear of drugs and alcohol.

Also in 1963, a new kind of state hospital was opened in Haverford, Pennsylvania. Haverford is south of Philadelphia in Delaware County. The facility was built on two hundred and thirty acres. Officials wanted to get away from the warehouse model of care and wanted to actually treat and possibly cure the patients. The staff used art and pet therapies, held patient get-togethers and other treatments to socialize them so they could eventually enter the Chester and Delaware County suburbs of Philadelphia.

Sophie was a young teenager in 1963 and lived not too far from Haverford Hospital. I could not help but wonder if she was ever there.

I grew up in the Somerton section of Northeast Philadelphia, just minutes from Byberry Hospital. We had to drive past the haunted-looking buildings to get anywhere. My father told us when we were very young that this was the place they sent the "bad" people. People that were so bad they couldn't even be sent to jail. The older kids in our neighborhood delighted in telling the younger kids frightening accounts of brains being fried and Frankenstein monsters being created.

It was no wonder when my Girl Scout leader announced we would be taking a trip to Byberry to sing Christmas songs to the poor crazy people that I nearly vomited.

When our bus pulled up to the large old brick building, I noticed a new sign over the double doors. "Outpatient Services" the white sign with stark black letters read. I may have only been ten years old, but I knew what that sign meant. They were letting the "bad" people go. I was terrified.

I was already a weird kid, and I knew that. I was afraid of airplanes. I was sure they all carried bombs and were going to drop them on us. That thought was doubly frightening for me because my father worked for Eastern Airlines and was based at the Philadelphia International Airport. I remember my stomach hurting every time he had to go to work. I sort of felt safe from the bombs in school because they taught us what to do there.

At home, I was scared to look people in the eye because I knew I would be able to feel their pain, their happiness, or their evilness. I was scared to sleep because in my dreams, my dead grandmother spoke to me. I was afraid to look the crazy people in the eyes because I did not want to know or to feel their pain. It made me feel helpless because I was a just a kid. As much as I wanted to help, I had no idea what to do to help.

I did not have one friend in this Girl Scout group. It was intentional. I didn't like any of them. At this moment, walking down this long sidewalk with a frigid wind pelting my bare legs, I wished I would have thought to make at least one friend. It would have been comforting to have a hand to squeeze and then to have mine squeezed back. I had no doubt we were all walking into a real-life horror movie. I took small comfort in the fact the rest of the group looked scared to death as well, including the troop leader and the two mothers who were chaperones. I could feel their fear.

I hoped it was warm inside. I started saying Hail Marys and asked Mary to please keep us safe and not let any crazy people chase us—or worse, axe us to death.

The stench of ammonia burned our noses as soon as the large double doors were closed behind us. Some loud and some very distant moaning could be heard, as well as the occasional hair-standing straight-up-bloodcurdling screams. We were standing in a foyer, waiting. The floors were recently mopped. I recognized the dried swirly residue left behind when you mop a too-dirty floor with a too-dirty mop. I recognized it because my mother was a last-minute cleaner. She could dust, vacuum, and mop the entire house in the twenty minutes before my father was due home from work. There were always swirls of residue left behind when she was finished.

This was one time I was grateful to be so tall and thin. When we were led into some sort of hall, the troop leader told me to stand in the back row against the wall. There was a woman with a gray disheveled bun sitting in a chair, clapping her hands and shaking her head up and down. There was a short man with a green wool scarf wrapped around his neck and wearing pajamas. He was sitting in the corner, facing the wall, and rocking his body vigorously back and forth. A tall, thin man wearing plaid pants and a bright-red T-shirt was smiling at me. I tried not to look in his eyes, but I did. He was inching closer and closer to where I was standing. Just as I was about to jump out of my skin, a nurse appeared and shuffled him back to his seat. I forced myself to look at the floor, the ceiling, or one of the two nurses in the room. Some of the patients laughed uncontrollably, some screamed, some cried, and a few sat motionless, staring into space.

I was so relieved when the last chorus of "Make New Friends" was finished, and the nurses thanked us for visiting. Getting out of there was all I could think about. I wondered how one could make sure they never *caught* a mental illness because I was going to start doing whatever it took immediately.

What I saw that day was horrific. I had vivid nightmares for at least ten years. Sometimes I still have them now.

Shortly after that visit to Byberry, my cousins and I were playing in the woods by my grandmother's house in Somerton. Byberry road zigzags, and at one point, where it ends is an elementary school, the Comly School. I went to kindergarten there. Beside and behind the school was a small patch of woods. Byberry road reconnected on the other side of the woods. I am not sure why, but we called those woods the pork chop woods.

One Sunday afternoon, my cousins and me were playing hide-and-seek behind the school. It was my turn to be "it," so I walked slowly, trying to peer through the trees out of the corners of my eyes while also keeping my eyes on the ground so I could pay attention to where I was walking. My male cousins loved to scare me, so I was anticipating them jumping out from somewhere behind me and screaming. I thought I heard someone moving in front of me. I looked up and saw a man. He was three feet in front of me.

He had shoulder-length golden hair and gorgeous brown eyes. He looked to me like a rock star. He looked like one of the guys my babysitter showed me on an album cover. Maybe he was a movie or a TV star. At the same time I was trying to figure out what he was, I realized he was naked, and I realized I could not move. I was paralyzed with fear. Out of the corner of my eye, I saw my two cousins standing about fifteen feet away. I gasped. The man was smiling as he walked closer to me. He did not appear aggressive and in fact, he seemed harmless. My cousins were boys, ten and eleven. I was ten. He stood right in front of me. I kept my eyes on his eyes and his hands. I did not want to look down. He asked me if I wanted to touch him. What seemed harmless at first suddenly became terrifying. A little voice from deep down in my belly got very loud and said run. I prayed that my cousins were running with me. The three of us ran, screaming at the top of our lungs until we could not breathe. We collapsed on the ground and realizing we were back at the playground with people around, we started laughing hysterically.

We never said one word to our grandparents or parents. I am quite sure this man was one of the patients released from the hospital. He was most likely living in those woods, which did lead to the Byberry grounds. Not a day goes by that I do not realize how different that encounter could have been. I wonder how many other children playing in the pork chop woods had encounters with this man or other "strangers." Were they as lucky as we had been? Was that man one of the orphans of the state that grew up irreversibly broken?

We never went back into those woods again.

After that incident, whenever we drove past the hospital, I would crouch down in the back of the car. I did not want to look out the window and see that naked man standing there at the bus stop on the corner of Bustleton and Byberry Roads.

I do not think anyone talked about sexual abuse of any kind back then. Perhaps they did, but I never heard any one mention it. I knew Byberry housed some of the country's most notorious criminally insane. I wandered and still wonder how many of them were child molesters and rapists. I wonder why no one warned us that such people existed.

Four out of five women in my immediate circle have had some sort of experience like the one I had in those woods that day. Some of their experiences were much worse. Was this a direct result of letting hopelessly broken people out of institutions across the country? I believe it is.

Most institutions flew under the radar during the 1970s. Our country's attention was focused on the changing culture, war, and dirty politics. In the 1980s, the facilities were front and center once again. Reports of physical and sexual abuse ran rampant. Staff members were threatened but nothing changed.

In 1987, Pennsylvania governor Robert Casey ordered a blue ribbon committee (the political action used to stall for time) to investigate the charges. The committee announced the Philadelphia State Hospital had resisted reform from the very beginning. Four aides were fired (not charged with assault) for abuse and the facility was ordered to begin the process of closing its doors. Officials were told to release the least sick of the patients into the community. Four hundred patients were released that year. Some did well, some victimized others, and some became victims of crimes. That blue ribbon panel was asked to come up with an aftercare plan. Their plan was to create smaller group homes run by facilitators and overseen by the state. There was no money for these plans, so they pretty much were failures on delivery.

Where were these patients supposed to go? Many were elderly and had lived shackled most of their lives. In Northeast Philadelphia and in communities across America, severely ill people were roaming the streets of our communities. This is what created our country's homeless problem and our mental health crisis.

In April of 1988, patients and/or family members of patients began filing lawsuits that demanded care after being released from Byberry. By 1989, groups were banding together and filing class action suits. The groups demanded fifty million dollars.

The Blue Ribbon Coalition suggested more time was needed to put the wanted aftercare plans in place. In the meantime, more and more abuse was being reported. In August of 1989, a patient was found dead on the Byberry grounds. A week later, another was found dead, and a third attempted suicide.

That fall, a released patient froze to death on the property. Officials urged immediate closure of the institution. Still

Governor Casey insisted on closing the facility the correct way. By October, there were two hundred patients remaining in Byberry. They were receiving no care and no treatment.

Finally, in February of 1990, the budget of fifty million dollars for aftercare was approved.

The money was used to open smaller scale residence houses that offered twenty-four-hour care along with treatment. The homes were staffed with displaced workers from Byberry. Patient care was to be monitored by consumer agencies that were paid by the state—the same system used by the Philadelphia Child Protective Agency that had failed miserably, even causing the death of an innocent little girl, probably more.

While there is no doubt in anybody's mind that Byberry Hospital needed to close its doors, it was sad that some of the patients within its dark, moldy walls were receiving by far the best, most up-to-date treatments available by the country's most respected doctors. The buildings were wrought with guinea pigs, and a lot of the experimental therapies and medications were working. There was great concern over what would happen to "these" patients as they seemed to be nearly cured. We know that one such young woman went on to die of suicide.

Byberry Hospital closed its doors for the last time in June of 1990. The property was pretty much abandoned until a developer recently built a fifty-five-plus community on the grounds. I don't know why that upsets me so much, but it does.

I believe wholeheartedly that those human beings that were tortured within the walls of Byberry and every other asylum in the world deserved love, compassion, and the most up-to-date treatment and care. Why couldn't we make those hospitals safe places to do that for them? Why did people think if they couldn't monitor what went on in the confines of a hospital that they were going to monitor what happened with these people in the communities? Why did people think that in order to protect the rights of one person, putting that person's safety and the safety of entire communities at risk was okay?

~

Named for Eunice Kennedy, the mission of the NICHD is to ensure that every person is born healthy and wanted, that women suffer no harmful effects from reproductive processes, and that all children have the chance to achieve their full potential for healthy and productive lives, free from disease or disability, and to ensure the health, productivity, independence, and well-being of all people through optimal rehabilitation.

The NICHD has made revolutionary progress toward achieving its goals. Since the institute was founded, they have accomplished the following:

- Infant death rates in the United States have dropped more than 70 percent, with much of this decline resulting from NICHD-sponsored research.

- Survival rates for respiratory distress syndrome have gone from 5 percent in the 1960s to 95 percent today, due to advances in respirator technologies and the availability of replacement lung surfactant, resulting from the research efforts of the NICHD and other institutes.

- The rate of sudden infant death syndrome has dropped by 50 percent since the NICHD-led Back to Sleep, an education campaign to reduce the risk of SIDS began.

- Transmission of HIV from infected mother to fetus and infant has dropped from 25 percent to less than 1 percent, as a result of NICHD's efforts in collaboration with other agencies and organizations.

- The incidence of haemophilus influenzae type B (Hib), once the leading cause of acquired IDDs, has dropped more than 99 percent, because of development of the

Hib vaccine by NICHD scientists, which has nearly eliminated this disease.

- Phenylketonuria, a disorder that also caused IDDs in many individuals, has been successfully eliminated as a factor in cognitive development through newborn screening and dietary therapy. Congenital hypothyroidism, once responsible for many cases of IDDs, no longer has an impact on cognitive development because of screening techniques used to detect the condition in all newborns in time to allow treatment to prevent its effects.

- Infertility that at one time kept couples from having babies of their own often can be treated and reversed.

- Sound scientific information about the safety and effectiveness of different contraceptive methods for women and men is now available.

- Many social, physical, and behavioral rehabilitation treatments for people with mental, developmental, and physical disabilities are now available.

14

Are We All Crazy

Whether we agree with the way President Kennedy opened the gates and let the mentally ill out of the state institutions without a solid plan for aftercare or not, we must agree that the conversation about the care and treatment of our mentally ill and intellectually challenged was started by him, his administration and his family.

President Kennedy and his family forever changed public attitudes toward people with intellectual disabilities. Their influence on related policies and programs can still be seen today. In the years following the Kennedy administration, the Congress has passed 116 acts or amendments providing support for people with intellectual disabilities and their families.

The Mental Health Act of 1966 mandated as many patients as possible in institutions across the country to be released back into the communities. Upon their release, they were given a new suit of clothes, twenty-five dollars and an appointment with a community mental health center. More than 350,000 patients were released from state hospitals into the surrounding communities between 1965 and 1980. Less than 1 percent of them showed up for their follow-up appointments.

Public attitudes and policy may have been changed forever but President Kennedy's reason for wanting to change those attitudes and the country's policies in the first place was because of his sister, Rosemary, and believe it or not, she never left the institution.

Many other state mental hospitals were closed around the same time Byberry Hospital was closed. Most of them are nothing more now than extremely frightening Halloween attractions.

The Danvers State Hospital in rural Massachusetts opened in 1878 as a self-contained psychiatric hospital. It is rumored to be the hospital where the first prefrontal lobotomy was performed. A lobotomy is a surgical procedure that involves severing connections in the brain's frontal lobe. The frontal lobe is targeted because that is the part of the brain associated with personality and behavior. It is an umbrella term for a series of operations in which surgeons damage brain tissue to treat damaged brains. The treatment was invented at a time when people were desperate for some sort of intervention. The procedure has always been controversial, yet it was widely used for more than two decades.

The procedure was reported as a successful treatment for depression, schizophrenia, panic disorder and mania but also had severe side effects. Many patients lost bowel and bladder control, had eye problems, severe weight gain, apathy and lethargy.

In 1945, a procedure was developed to enter the frontal lobe through the eye sockets. This particular procedure involved a modified ice pick and a hammer. Shockingly, it was not considered a surgical procedure and was often performed in mental institutions by unqualified psychiatrists.

Approximately fifty thousand lobotomies were performed in the United States. Only a small percentage of people improved. Most patients lost the ability to function on their own.

Critics believe lobotomies were performed on unruly patients in overcrowded institutions as a way to maintain control. In the novel and the movie adaption of *One Flew Over the Cuckoo's Nest*, that is what happens to the character Randall Patrick Murphy played by Jack Nicolson. The lobotomy leaves him mute and lifeless. The movie is considered to be an unexaggerated, realistic portrayal of what went on in our state run asylums.

These days, our mental health patients can be made lethargic with medication alone.

Danvers was originally built as a residential treatment facility to care for the mentally ill. It expanded in 1889 to include a nursing school and a pathological research lab in 1895. In the 1920s, the facility was used to test the mental development of children. The hospital began closing in the 1960s with the last of the buildings on the campus closing in 1992.

Most of the buildings have been renovated and are now apartments.

Bridgewater State Hospital, also in Massachusetts, is a state facility for the criminally insane and for those whose sanity is being evaluated by the criminal justice system. It opened as a home for the poor in 1885. The facility has been the subject of a 1967 documentary, *Titicut Follies*.

By the 1970s, the property had four separate facilities—the hospital for the criminally insane, a hospital for the sexually dangerous, a center for alcoholics and a minimum-security prison.

This facility like most others was investigated over the years for its cruel treatment of inmates. This facility was also investigated for keeping inmates long after their sentences expired. A study in 1968 showed that at least thirty inmates had been committed to the hospital illegally.

Albert DeSalvo, the Boston Strangler, was an inmate at Bridgewater until he escaped in 1967. When he was recaptured, he was transferred to a maximum-security prison.

In 1968, it was discovered that there were 250 forgotten men who were housed at Bridgewater for over twenty five years, long after their original sentences expired.

Bridgewater is still in operation today. In 2009, a patient died after being illegally restrained. His family was awarded three million dollars and Governor Deval Patrick ordered an investigation into the practices at the facility.

In 2014, the Boston Globe did an exposé on how the use of forced restraints actually increased over the five years following the death of that inmate. After the exposé, the governor publicly reprimanded the prison administration for their attempts to cover up procedural wrongdoings, including the continued use of the restraints that resulted in the death.

Another inmate who was excessively restrained and secluded had his civil suit settled out of court. That man had never even been convicted of a crime. I'm guessing Bridgewater's days are numbered, finally.

They recently built a fifty-five-plus housing development on the old Byberry grounds. I was honesty shocked. I want to drive through the neighborhood yelling, "Do you know what you are living on top of? Are you all crazy?"

The mental health hospital located in Delaware County where Sophie grew up, Haverford State Hospital, was considered a jewel in the mental health field when it opened in 1962. It was intended to house 575 patients. Shortly after opening, the institution housed more than seven hundred. The facility continuously failed state inspections.

The closing in 1997 of that hospital put close to five hundred Delaware County residents out of work and about the same number of mentally ill patients into group homes or released directly into the surrounding Delaware and Chester County communities.

Our mentally ill citizens now have rights. They should have rights. Who would argue that point? Remember one of these rights is to decide for themselves whether or not they are mentally ill. Is there any sane person that sees any sort of logic in that statement?

It makes me think of the time I had a severe concussion. I knew my thoughts and actions were crazy. I knew they were crazy, but I could not make my mind make a decision to do something about the craziness. I knew I needed help but could not make myself form the words. It came out as anger, which was so not my personality. The best way to explain it is, I was stuck in my own head. I wondered if it was like that for the mentally ill. Do they realize their thoughts and actions are not sensible, but they are stuck the way I was? If so, how cruel that we give them the responsibility of trying to figure out what the next step is when they are incapable of thinking past where they are.

Again, we need to stop putting the rights of one person above their own safety, as well as the rights and safety of many.

I think of that amusement ride, the ship, that swings dramatically to one side and stays there for a minute and then quickly swings completely to the other side. This is how drastically the treatment of our mentally ill has changed in this country over the last fifty years. We can never go back to the barbaric treatment of these human beings, but we must come up with something.

Because our city, state and federal government could not get it together to manage these asylums, they simply gave up and opened the doors and let more than a million mentally ill people into our communities with no homes to go to and no hope for continued treatment. Whoever pulled that plug is the one that single-handedly created our country's homeless and mental health problem.

That problem continues to grow with the downturn of the economy. Now there are thousands of families with children that are homeless. Returning military personal, the elderly and recently released criminals are adding thousands upon thousands more to the homeless count in the United States.

It is now an epidemic in America and the numbers of homeless people will only continue to grow. Giving states, counties and municipalities money to open shelters is not working. I feel we need to go back to the time when traditional family takes care of family. Families must be given the right to "measure" whether their loved one is at risk of hurting themselves or others. I understand this is a slippery slope and opens the door for revenge, lawsuits and more, but the line must be drawn somewhere. Our country cannot continue on this unethical path. Perhaps we should look to our third-world neighbors and examine how they treat their elderly family members.

As it is now, if you threaten to do harm to yourself or another person or someone's property, you may or may not be taken to the closest hospital where they may or may not keep you for twenty-four to seventy-two hours, which is usually decided by insurance companies and the mentally ill person. Family members are left to keep running on the hamster wheel until they finally throw their hands up in the air in total frustration and put the helpless mentally ill relative out on the street.

A schoolteacher, Dorothea Dix (1802–1887) was one of the first advocates for the humane care of the mentally ill. She is credited with establishing at least thirty-two state mental health hospitals in the United States.

For her, it started in 1841 when she visited a Boston jail to teach a Sunday school class.

What she found there were hardened criminals, feebleminded children, and mentally ill prisoners being kept together unsegregated in inhumane conditions. She immediately fought for a court order to have heat turned on in the jail. The cause became her lifelong passion. She started by visiting other jails, asylums and hospitals and carefully documenting her findings.

She read the available literature on mental illness and what was known back then as emotional disease. She made herself an expert on the work of Benjamin Rush, William Tuke and Philippe Pinel, who were well-known reformers.

She was the author of several books on teaching and of children's books, and the royalties from those works afforded her the funds to travel in order to do research. By 1850, Ms. Dix had raised enough support from influential and prominent citizens that bills were introduced to the Congress that would provide the states with the necessary funds to create or improve facilities for the mentally ill. The bills passed both houses in 1851 but were vetoed by President Pierce on the legal ground that our mentally ill citizens were the responsibility of their own states, not the federal government.

Ms. Dix also visited asylums in England, Ireland and Europe. After finding deplorable conditions at an asylum in the city of Rome, Ms. Dix demanded and was granted an audience with Pope Pius IX. Can you imagine? I would have loved meeting her. The pope compared her and her work to that of Mother Theresa. She used her influence wherever she went to publicize the poor conditions of the mentally ill and in advocating for improved care.

She spent her final years as a resident guest at the Trenton State Hospital in New Jersey, a psychiatric hospital founded through her efforts.

How sad that the politicians and people before us took the institutions built from that woman's heartfelt passion, empathy and hard work and allowed them to become exactly what she fought so hard her entire life to prevent—torture chambers.

How sad is it that still today in the twenty-first century, we cannot find treatments for mental health disorders with fewer side effects. How sad that we still don't realize that protecting the rights of one or a few can have devastating effects for whole communities. I do not like the idea of taking anyone's human rights from them, but there must be a safe, well-planned solution that benefits everyone.

The never-ending debating over the passing of and the enacting of the Affordable Care Act was going on in this country as I was doing the research for this book. The saying, "If you do not know your history, you are sure to repeat it," came to my mind as I read the eleven-hundred-page bill. Are we repeating bad history here? I was hoping with all of my heart that we were not, but my mind was and is still telling me we are headed for some bad history with this bill. The system needs changing without a doubt. I am just afraid this is not going to be the change any of us were hoping it would be.

Our health insurance industry is broken. Throwing eleven hundred pages of ideas out there and hoping a few of them stick is equivalent to opening the doors of the asylums and letting everyone out. It wasn't the answer then, and it is certainly not the answer today.

Credit has to be given to those certain people that fought so hard for the ACA for reasons other than political. Those politicians that have nothing but the best interest at heart for the American people when it comes to their health and well-being. If only we could get those like-minded politicians, leaving out their egos, on all sides of the aisle to sit down with our finest health care professionals, families, and advocates for the seriously ill, as well as those people and politicians with a financial stake in the outcome, like plan administrators and insurance company officials, I can only imagine the positive changes that could happen.

My biggest fear of the Affordable Health Care Act is that we are repeating bad history. Medicaid and Medicare, both systems designed with the absolute best intentions, have been plagued with fraud, mismanagement, poor leadership and lack of accountability since their inception. Our VA medical system is another example of our government's complete lack of credibility when it comes to providing and managing large-scale quality health care.

The problem with our nation's asylums was corrupt politics and a complete lack of leadership and accountability by the management and the staff. The problems began as soon as the facilities were opened back in Ben Franklin's days. Occasionally, newspapers would shine a light on the atrocities, action would be taken, and the guilty would be fired. Once the media attention died down the staff member was quietly rehired and the horrors continued.

The problems in our VA medical system are just as systemic, probably even worse than they were in those asylums. People are in danger of dying. I fear we are headed toward just opening the doors and releasing our veterans into the already-overwhelmed community health centers and the closing of our VA medical centers. Having our veterans treated at community health centers like everyone else sounds like a great idea. It even looks like a good quick fix until we look back into history and see how opening the doors of those asylums in the 1960s created the homeless and mental health crisis we are still not dealing with today.

Removing and replacing the leader of the VA administration was long overdue. It will not fix anything. Leaders need to be committed to quality, accountability and results. They need to create strategies and see that their teams are responsibly implementing those strategies. The teams working in our VA medical system are implementing a complete lack of respect and disregard for our country's heroes. They are there to collect a decent paycheck and government benefits. Nothing else is demanded of them.

Unfortunately, any attempt the new leader or any subsequent leaders may make at requiring correctible action and accountability from employees will be complicated by union leaders that will completely cripple any attempt at change he might make. Chances are, it will be business as usual again in no time. Add to that those narcissistic, stagnant politicians on *all* sides offering endless, useless investigations that do nothing but rob taxpayers and fatten their own wallets.

The problem that needs to be "fixed" is the union "leader" problem we have in this country. While unions were started for many valid reasons, they have since done exactly what they were supposed to do. We now have government employee protection agencies and laws to protect our workers from abuse, discrimination, unsafe conditions and more. Unions are a waste of hardworking employee's money. Because most of these unions are hanging on by a thread, the leaders are becoming desperate and looking for ways to "money grab."

Not all union leaders are bad people, but the few that are "bad" certainly give the entire concept of unionism a bad name. Unions are just another example of corruption that has gone on for so long it would be nearly impossible to eradicate it from the system.

The Affordable Care Act has opened the doors to let everybody in. Again, on paper, that looks like a good idea, but in reality, it is going to collapse along with other completely broken systems.

I fear we are repeating some very, very bad history here. I am not trying to make any political statements. I am just wondering what all of us are thinking. Are we thinking at all? Are we all crazy?

15

The Lump

I started to remind Sophie at eight thirty in the morning that she had to take a shower. She smiled and said she would take one later. You have to shower today, I told her again and again. After my own shower, I placed the plastic safety chair into the tub and put a towel on the seat to make it softer for her to sit on and not as cold. I put four fresh towels on the counter and a washcloth on the arm of the shower chair. A bath sheet worked better on the floor than the tiny bath mat, so I folded the mat and put it in the hall closet. I lined up the mouthwash, baby powder, Q-tips and facial moisturizer on the sink, doubting she would use any of the products.

I ran downstairs and into Sophie's room and picked out an outfit for her to wear. I chose a pair of mint-green linen pants and a cream-colored tank and sweater set. If only I could talk her into wearing real shoes. The plastic slides she wore made me cringe. At least I was able to talk her into wearing socks so her feet wouldn't get frostbite. The socks with the slides looked absolutely ridiculous. That was a fight I chose not to start. Cream pumps or flats would be so cute with this outfit. Even white or cream sneakers would be adorable. She only had white and black socks. I chose the white. Would she ever wear knee-highs, I wondered. I wanted to throw away those stupid plastic shoes so badly. If she didn't dig through our trash cans, I could probably get away with throwing them out and letting her think she lost them. I realized how mean that would be, or would it be? Plastic shoes cannot be healthy for your feet.

Her toenails were disgusting too. I tried to cut them for her once, but she screamed so loud I had no choice but to stop. When people age, their toenails thicken and harden naturally. The thickening can also be caused by a fungus, other disease, a trauma and of course, improper fitting shoes. In Sophie's case, it could have been all of these. I tried talking her into seeing a podiatrist but she wanted nothing to do with that idea. I could only imagine the screaming she would do and how embarrassed I would be.

Moving on, I quickly scrambled an egg and cooked it in the microwave for her. I generously buttered her soft toast and poured a large glass of apple juice and put everything on the dining room table for her. She begged me to let her eat in the recliner. It was another fight I chose not to start. I moved the meal to her end table and placed a dishtowel on her lap.

I ran back upstairs to gather some laundry.

"Deena, Deena," she shrieked.

I yelled down to her asking her what she needed.

"You forgot me peas in my eggies," she whined.

I could not tell her we did not have any because I had enough canned peas in the cupboard to wait out Armageddon. Why did I think she would be okay without peas for that one day? I ran downstairs, opened a can of peas and drained the liquid off of them. I put a few spoonfuls of peas into a small bowl. I placed the bowl in the microwave. The smell of microwave eggs is bad enough first thing in the morning. Adding the smell of nasty canned peas and that slimy liquid they come in is so gross.

The smell gets stuck in your nostrils and stays there. Taking the small bowl out of the microwave and then lifting it with a paper towel, I walked over to the recliner. Carefully, I scooped the peas from the bowl and piled them onto her plate. I asked her to take her plate into the kitchen when she was finished eating. She smelled so badly I had to fight my gag reflex. I could not wait to get her into the shower.

I put a load of laundry into the washer adding extra Tide liquid and Downy fabric softener because I knew it would make the house smell better. It wouldn't get to the root of the odor problem, but for right then, I needed that putrid eggy, peas and urine smell to be gone.

I know odors make me nauseous, but I wondered if just smelling something gross could actually make you physically sick. We breathe ten thousand to twenty thousand liters of oxygen every day. Odors can alert us that there is something that may be harmful to us. The good news is that we are able to smell even dangerous chemicals long before they are at a level high enough to be a risk to our health.

Some people are simply more sensitive to odors than others. That would be lucky me. Younger people, nonsmokers and women, especially pregnant women, seem to be the most sensitive. Most people are bothered more by smells in the morning and on an empty stomach.

Certain chemicals are harmful and yes, they can cause us health problems. It is the chemical not the odor that causes the health risk. Some harmful chemicals are regulated by the Environmental Protection Agency, or EPA, under the Clean Air Act. Other environmental chemical odors may not be regulated under the Clean Air Act, thus making it very difficult to address and/or enforce nuisance odor-type complaints. Just because something smells bad does not mean it is harmful to the health of humans or animals. Rotten eggs cannot make you dangerously ill. They can cause odor-sensitive people to feel sick to their stomachs, to gag, a headache, scratchy throat and even itchy, burning eyes.

Bad smells raise my level of anxiety and can ruin my good mood. It is difficult to determine where the line is between nuisance odors and outright public health risks. If untreated human waste is considered a health risk. Wouldn't Sophie's peeing all over herself and our furniture be considered a risk to her health and ours?

Sophie had asked me for some cornstarch a few days earlier. I had no idea why she wanted it but it ended up all over her room. The silky powder was caked on her bathroom floor and in the sink. I wondered how it got wet. Was she using it to mask odor? Scrubbing her room and that bathroom was not in my plans for that day but it had to be done. Against my own better judgment, I asked her how the starch ended up all over the floor. Her answer to me was she used too much. While I was vacuuming the sticky white powder that was thickly caked in her carpet, I decided Sophie was going to start wearing bladder control briefs. Enough was enough. I was not going to risk our health because it was uncomfortable for me to insist she wear Depends. Convincing her she needed them would not be easy, but I had no choice. She had to be convinced. If you have a problem and there is a solution, opting for the solution is always the best idea.

I continued to remind her throughout the day that she had to get into the bathtub. I was getting angry. She had not moved from the recliner in hours. I decided I needed some fresh air and a break, so I went to the CVS to pick up some Depends for her. She whined about me going to the store, but she would not come with me.

The briefs came in all sorts of colors and styles and honestly, they were not that bad looking. I hoped Sophie would see it that way and not fight me. She was not going to have a choice. If I had to, I would have John tell her it was something she had to do for sanitary reasons. I took my time, slowly walking up and down each aisle, just looking. I picked up a couple of scented candles. I knew again they would not solve the problem, but they would help. I looked for some sort of cream that Sophie could use instead of cornstarch. I figured she most likely had a urinary tract infection and that was causing her irritation. It was so frustrating that she refused to take antibiotics. I found an antibiotic cream, and I picked up some cranberry apple juice hoping she would at least try it.

Once back at the house, I sat and watched the soaps with her. A commercial came on for Depends. I blurted out excitedly that I just bought them for her. It worked. I think she was confused and thought the soap stars were talking about wearing them. Whatever she thought, I was happy it worked. I was so relieved. I put my foot down and insisted she take her shower once the next show ended. I promised to stay in the bathroom with her while she showered. I hoped if the fear of falling was the reason she hated to wash, she would feel safe with me close.

She walked up the steps ahead of me, whining the entire time about how much it hurt her legs to walk up the steps. I told her if it hurt that bad, she would let me take her to the doctors and let him help her. She turned around and with her most evil eyes and voice, she said, "They ain't gonna cut me."

I told her they would most likely give her a prescription for some medication to help with the pain.

"It make me stupid," she screamed.

It was so hard not to get angry with her. I wanted to scream, *You are stupid*, and immediately felt so guilty for wanting to yell at her. She was right. Pain medication does make you stupid.

We went into the bathroom, which is rather small. I sat on the toilet. Sophie just stood there. I got up and turned the shower on for her. I reached up and directed the shower head where I thought the water would roll off Sophie's back. Water rolled down the underside of my arm. I told her to get undressed and get into the tub.

"It's dirty," she cried.

"It is not dirty," I told her.

She said she did not like the ugly shower chair; she did not want to get undressed in front of me along with a long list of other excuses. I told her I would put my head under the towel so I wouldn't be able to see her. I was getting angry and amused at the same time. I put the towel over my head and could not believe what she did. She bent over the tub, which was interesting since a few minutes before, she could barely walk up the steps. She wet her hair under the running water and grabbed a towel and claimed she was done. I felt so stupid. This crazy woman had not taken an actual bath or shower the whole time she lived here. I was furious. I ripped the towel off my head and told her in my firmest voice to get into that tub immediately before I called John.

She screamed, "Nooo, me done already me clean."

"Get in that tub right now," I demanded, fighting tears of frustration and stupidity.

She climbed into the tub and sat on the chair. I reminded her to use the grab bars.

I took the washcloth, squeezed some liquid Dove soap onto it, and held it under the warm water. Dove has the cleanest smell and it leaves your skin smelling so good long after a shower. I should have known she was faking showers because she never smelled like Dove when she came downstairs. What an idiot I had been. I handed the washcloth to Sophie and told her to start washing herself. I reached over her head for the shampoo bottle and squirted too much on her hair. I gagged and started washing her hair. She would not lay her head back, so I got a cup from the sink, filled it with warm water and poured it over her head, taking care not to get any of the water in her eyes. The whole time, she was screaming, swatting at me and trying to push me away.

I just kept saying over and over again in the most mundane voice I could muster, "Sophie, I am so sorry, but you have to be clean. You cannot live here if you do not take care of yourself. I am just trying to help you. We want you to stay here, but you have to be clean. I promise I do not want to, and I will never hurt you. I want to help you."

She finally started to calm down. I continued to tell her to relax and enjoy the warm water.

"Doesn't it feel good?" I asked her. "Warm water is really good for aches and pains from being karate chopped," I whispered to her.

The clean scent of the Dove and Sophie finally calming down helped me to relax. Smiling at her, I continued to gently wash her and rinse her with warm water. Then like the music of a great song suddenly stopping and my heart stopping with it, I felt something that shouldn't be there. It was a rock-hard lump right under her left shoulder blade. I froze. It took a few minutes to stop the pictures that were on fast-forward in my mind. Once I found my voice, I asked her if she knew it was there.

"Yes," she answered. Then as quickly as she said yes, she told me she did know it was there. Getting upset she started to yell again, "They not ever gonna cut me. I have to eat garwic so it go away."

"Sophie, we have to go to the doctors and see what this is," I pleaded with her. "I will not take no for an answer." I went back to my quiet voice, trying to calm her down again. "We will talk about this later."

I finished washing her, taking care not to miss an inch, knowing it may be a while before I could get her in the shower again. It was so hard not to cry and even harder to pretend that everything was okay.

Surprisingly, she put the cream and the Depend on with only a little bit of a fight but whined about putting the rest of her clothes on. I had a lump in my throat. It was dry and it hurt. I knew she had cancer. I was so sad for her. I helped her pull her shirt over her head and pull her pants up. I told her to sit on the toilet and I put her socks on for her. I towel dried her hair and reached for the hair dryer. Of course, she hated that and started to scream again. I spoke softly to her while I brushed, dried and styled her hair. She was either whining, screaming, or crying the entire time.

I was so glad that shower was over and happy that she was clean, but what a day. I was exhausted. Realizing that we had been conned by her made me angry. Realizing she had no real shower in over a year made me feel so sick to my stomach. Honestly, I felt so stupid for not putting it all together sooner. Her hair was always soaking wet and more than dripping.

We went downstairs. I covered her with a fluffy blanket and made her a nice warm dinner. We watched soaps together until John came home from work at nine. I did not want to tell him about her never taking an actual shower, and I really did not want to tell him about the lump I found. It always felt like I was complaining to him about Sophie. Maybe I was complaining, but I also felt like he needed to know the reality. He needed to accept the fact that Sophie was not well, and it was likely she would never be able to take care of herself or live on her own again. I felt so bad, so afraid for her. How would John take this news?

John picked the TV remote up from Sophie's end table and sat on the big red sofa. I decided to come out with it right then and not wait until we were alone. Right in front of Sophie, I told him, "While I was helping Sophie get a shower today, I felt a lump under her shoulder blade. I think she needs to go to the doctors as soon as possible to have it checked out." And then knowing it was a lie, I said, "It's probably nothing, but better safe than sorry."

All John had to do after I blurted it out was look at Sophie and, raising his voice slightly, said, "You are going to see the doctor about that lump, and you are going to do whatever he advises you to do, and you will do it as soon as possible."

She put her head down and whimpered, "Okay, John, me go to see my dokker."

I wished I tried that trick with her months ago.

Relieved that, that was easier than I thought it would be, my mind wondered to why Sophie sometimes spoke like a sweet two-year-old and at other times like an angry old woman. Her friend Lisa told me she could never figure that out either. She said Sophie had been doing it for as long as she had known her. Was it a habit? Was it possible she couldn't help herself?

Was baby talk a symptom of a mental illness? Sophie was overwhelmed with fear and worry. Quite often, she looked sad and depressed. Her thinking was often confused. She also had trouble sleeping, paranoia, and was distanced from her family. I knew those could be considered symptoms of a mental illness or disorder, but I couldn't find any reference to baby talking adults and a mental health condition. It didn't always annoy me but at times, it did get on my nerves.

I decided to hold off on telling John about her fake showers for a while. It just seemed like it would be mean to pile on, to gang up on her at that time. I was actually proud of myself that I discovered her hoax and that I did what had to be done and got her clean. I also realized I was going to have to put her in the shower myself for as long as she was here in this house.

The next morning, I called Sophie's doctor's office and made an appointment. The soonest appointment I could get was for the following week. They seemed to know over the phone exactly who Sophie was. I was relieved about that. I was not looking forward to that appointment. I knew a biopsy would be happening, and I did not even want to imagine how horrible that would be for her. I also knew how embarrassing it would be for me to be the one to take her to the hospital and have her screaming like a two-year-old throughout the whole procedure.

I wished I had asked her more about her friend, the one that died from cancer. No wonder the poor thing was so terrified of surgery and a cancer diagnosis. She saw the horrible side effects of treatment up close and personal. In the case of her friend, not all of the discomfort, sickness, and pain she went through had a happy ending.

She also watched her sister-in-law get sick, go through treatments, and still end up in Fair Acres suffering and eventually dying. I didn't know what else to do, so I prayed for her. Then I did what everyone including doctors tell you not to do. I Googled "shoulder blade lumps." Most of the information that came up was about something called a lipoma. Lipomas are soft lumps of fatty tissue. There was also information on cysts. A cyst should be able to be moved easily under the skin. Neither of these described Sophie's lump. Her lump was the size of, as round as, and as hard as a golf ball. Round lumps are not consistent with any type of muscle or bone injury. Calcium deposits could be hard to the touch but are usually not round. There was a Google image that looked exactly like Sophie's lump, but there was no information explaining what it was. The imagination tape in my head tried desperately to make this lump everything but what I knew in my gut it was.

It was going to be a long week. I was already stressing about having to force Sophie to take another shower before going to her doctor. There was no way I was going to be embarrassed by bringing a smelly, dirty woman into a professional office.

The next day, I asked Sophie if she ever went to any other doctor. She shook her head no and went back to watching her soaps. I pressed her.

"Did you ever go to a psychiatrist?"

"Me not crazy," she said without taking her eyes off of the TV.

"How about an eye doctor?" I asked.

"Me eyes are always perfect. I see everything."

That time, she glared at me as she answered. I knew that sarcasm was all I was going to get from her. It was time to find something else to keep my mind off of the *C* word.

I drove to Bristol and picked up my granddaughters Allyson and Julia. They were old enough to take care of themselves, so having them wouldn't be stressful—so I thought. They weren't here long when they decided they had enough of Sophie's soap operas. They took the remote and put on the Disney channel.

"Me don't like this stupid show," she whined at them. "You mean, stupid girls," she whispered under her breath.

That night up in my bedroom, I told the girls that I thought Sophie was sick, and I wanted them to be extra nice to her. I thought they were old enough to know that sometimes the elderly can be forgetful, and when they can't remember, it frightens them and they can lash out at the people closest to them. I didn't give them any details about the lump or that I suspected it was cancer. The next day, they drew pictures of hearts, flowers, and trees for her. They poured her apple juice and watched *The Young and The Restless* with her. They couldn't have been any sweeter. Sophie was suspicious, but when the girls didn't let up, she finally started to soften around them. I was so proud of them.

Lance and Louie knew something was wrong too. I believe dogs have a sixth sense. They were practically trying to sit on Sophie's back, and when she wouldn't let them up on the chair with her, they would wrap themselves around her feet. When she got up out of the chair, which wasn't very often, the dogs followed her. I also have no doubt these dogs have empathy. Louie has asthma, and whenever he has an attack, Lance runs around him, crying. He also finds John or me and cries until we follow him and help Louie. They can definitely tell if I am sad, worried, or hurt.

Dogs also know when we are scared. Certain breeds will protect their owners when they sense they are frightened. Not Lance and Louie, if I get scared, they get scared too. Their hair stands up on the back of their necks, and they shake. They hide behind my legs and try desperately to jump into my arms.

John came home from the dentist after having a root canal done and was having some pain, so I got him some Advil and told him to lie down on the big red sofa. The dogs started licking his mouth and crying. He had to go upstairs and shut the door because they wouldn't leave him alone.

Scientists believe dogs can actually smell cancer because of the chemical changes the cancer causes in the body. If your dog is paying particular attention to a certain part of your body, you should see your doctor.

16

Really Doctor?

Sophie's doctor's office was in an old blue house. There was no parking out in front of the building. It was located on a busier section of MacDade Boulevard. It wasn't easy to figure out how to get to the back of the building where there was a small parking lot. We drove around the block twice and finally saw the narrow driveway that led to the parking area. A walkway split and led to two different entrances. It was so confusing trying to figure out which door was the entrance to the doctor's office. Sophie seemed confused for a minute, and then she chose the path to the left. With blind faith, I followed.

"Me love me docker," she kept saying as we walked along the path to the front entrance. Sophie bent down and started to pick up some ugly-looking things that fell off of a tree and put them in her pocketbook. I told her they were dirty and she should leave them on the ground. I prayed there was no one that could see her. That warm flush of complete embarrassment came over me. She insisted loudly, she could wash them and eat them. They are black walnuts, she told me. She went on to say you could bake a pie with them or bake them, salt them and eat them.

Whatever, I thought. I needed to remember to throw them away when she was not paying attention so they did not attract bugs. I just got her smelling better and still needed to finish sanitizing the house. I did not need those ugly nuts lying around in her purse or in the house getting moldy.

The waiting room was full of people. We were able to find two chairs, but of course, they were right in the center of the room. At least these chairs were next to each other, I thought and then wondered why that would make me happy. Would I feel better if she was across the room where I could pretend I didn't know her? I asked Sophie if she would like a magazine to read. Surprisingly, she said yes, so I handed her one that had a soap opera star on the front cover. I walked into the next room and told the woman sitting behind a desk that Sophie was there. She asked for Sophie's medical card. I went back into the waiting room and helped Sophie find the cards in her bag. I was angry with myself for not making her take them out at home. I assumed they would have all of her information on file. It was embarrassing having those black walnuts falling out and rolling around on the floor. Most of the people in the waiting room were watching us. I was so uncomfortable. It felt like they were staring at us with compassion in their eyes, but it was still embarrassing.

We found the cards and I took them into the other room, which was actually a hallway with a desk up against the wall. I explained to the woman sitting behind the desk who I was and how I came to be taking care of Sophie. I told her I was trying to find a place for Sophie to live and asked her if she would ask the doctor if he would write a note saying Sophie was unable to take care of herself. I told her I did not want to ask the doctor in front of Sophie. The woman did not seem interested in me or my story at all. She told me to have a seat and they would call

Sophie back soon. I did not like her one bit. That woman's "We will call Sophie back soon" turned into a forty-five-minute wait.

Sophie like a two-year-old started acting out after fifteen minutes of waiting. I did my best to engage her in conversation about an article in the magazine she was reading. She was talking so loud. I decided to try to get her to tell me about the other times she came to see this doctor. She told me all of the women in the office were catty and rude, and she said it *so* loud. The other patients in the waiting room had trouble trying not to laugh. She went on to tell me how much she loved the doctor and that she knew he cared about her.

So far, her assessment of the women was spot on. I am so against any kind of girl-on-girl crime, and I knew without a doubt and could see with my own eyes that these women in this office did not care for Sophie one bit. I wondered how they could live with themselves.

Another woman, I guessed she was a nurse, came out and called Sophie's name. She ushered us into an examining room. We were sitting in there for at least twenty minutes when the first woman, the one from behind the desk, came into the room and asked me to come out to her desk. In the meantime, the nurse back in the examining room was trying to convince Sophie she needed to get her weight and vital signs. Hesitating, I stepped out to the desk. The woman said Sophie's medical card was expired and asked if I had a current one. I said no and told her I had no idea how to get a new one. The woman offered to call the assistance office to see if she could get them to fax over a new card. I told her I would appreciate her trying.

I went back into the examining room. The nurse asked me the reason for Sophie's visit. I always want to say something sarcastic when they ask that question because I know they have the reason for us being there with them in the notes. Instead,

I politely told her about the lump on Sophie's back. I also told her about the aches and pains she always seemed to be having and Sophie's lack of hygiene. I also mentioned Sophie needed a flu shot.

"I don't need no shot. No, no, no," she started screaming.

The nurse told Sophie to knock it off and told her she had been giving plenty of flu shots to people before this and she would be fine. The nurse's directness took me back a bit, but at the same time, I appreciated that. She seemed to know Sophie and knew how to deal with her. At the same time, I was a bit angry that she was so firm with Sophie. Would she speak to someone's child that aggressively? I doubted she would.

The woman from behind the desk came in to the examining room and said the assistance office was no help at all. She said we needed to pay sixty dollars for Sophie's visit and that we would have to go down to the assistance office in Chester and figure out how to resolve the Medicaid card issue. Sophie did not have sixty dollars in her pocketbook, and they would not take the walnuts as payment, so I handed over the cash and told Sophie she would have to reimburse me.

The doctor came into the tiny room and shook Sophie's hand and then mine. I introduced myself. He seemed to have a nice personality, but he was what some would call a "welfare doctor." I liked that he seemed patient with Sophie. He asked why she was there, and she put her head down and looked at the floor. I told him about the lump. He put his hand on her back, knowing right where the spot was.

"She's had this lump for a while. It is nothing," he said.

"Shouldn't she at least have it biopsied?" I asked him.

Sophie started saying repeatedly, "I don't want anyone cutting me."

He insisted it was nothing.

What the hell is he thinking? I thought.

The woman has an arm growing out of her back. I did not believe him, and I could not figure out if he wanted to avoid a scene with Sophie or he was dismissing her because of her circumstances.

I told him about all of her aches and pains and about the curled up fingers on her hand.

"That cannot be fixed," he said. "The muscles in her hand are dying."

Another idiotic thing, I thought. I had clients with this type of hand issue. They were prescribed splints and exercises to do to try to wake the muscles up or at least to keep them from getting worse. *What a quack this doctor was.* Then again, chances are Sophie probably wouldn't cooperate with any kind of therapy. I'm quite sure she wouldn't tolerate a splint.

He said he could prescribe a medication that would help her with her pain. He told her that she definitely had arthritis. I asked him if he treated her for the injuries she sustained in the storage unit attack. He said no. I told him Sophie told me she was karate chopped and that is what caused her hand to curl up that way and for her muscles to ache.

He said, "No, it wasn't caused by an injury. The pain she was experiencing was from arthritis."

He asked the nurse to see if they had any samples of the medication he was planning to prescribe for Sophie. The nurse came back into the room with a brown bag full of pills. I told Sophie she had to take them, or I was going to call the doctor and tell him. She promised the doctor and me she would take them.

He also insisted she take the flu shot. This doctor was more worried about Sophie getting the flu than he was about her dying of cancer. The nurse prepared the shot, and the doctor disappeared.

Sophie screamed like a maniac. "Me not need no shot!"

It was so embarrassing. That nurse was so angry she scared me. She told Sophie to stop screaming, and she took her arm and gave her the shot. Sophie cried like a two-year-old. I could not wait to get out of there. Once we were in the car, I asked Sophie if I could find her another doctor and she said no.

"Me love me docker," she whined.

He was a nice guy, but as far as any confidence in him medically, I had zero.

His lack of concern over the lump on Sophie's back bordered on malpractice. Either that or he knew Sophie wanted nothing to do with treatment, and he wasn't going to try to convince her because he didn't want to or because he knew it was a battle he would never win.

While we were out, I decided we should go to the social security office and get a copy of Sophie's social security card. It was another one of those chores that I knew would be a nightmare to complete, so I kept putting it off. I figured she would need her social security card to get her current Medicare and Medicaid cards. Honestly, I had no idea how any of it worked, but it seemed logical to get a copy of her social security card. I wanted to stop procrastinating and start getting things done. I wished the starting wasn't so uncomfortable.

She was whining on and off about the pain in her arm from the flu shot. That shot does make your muscles sore. I told her I had Advil in my purse, knowing she would never take one.

"Me be okay." Two minutes later, she was whining about it again.

The social security office was in Chester. Surprisingly, the building was not that hard to find. They had one of those ticket machines like the ones they have at the deli counter in supermarkets. I pulled a ticket from the machine and then found us two seats. I asked Sophie to find every identification card she had in her pocketbook. Again, the stupid walnuts along with rocks, stones and all sorts of other debris fell out of her purse and landed on the floor. The security guard was giving me the dirtiest looks. I wanted to smack him, but he was a pretty big guy. I smiled and shrugged my shoulders instead. Hadn't he ever seen a frail, helpless, mentally ill elderly person before? Some people really do have a low tolerance for crazy.

All Sophie really had in that mess of a bag to prove her identity was an expired medical card and a bunch of old junk mail. I tried to peek over at the junk mail to see the address on the envelope. It was the address of her friend Lisa's business, the one on MacDade Boulevard. Sophie called her Lisa, but her real name was Elyssa. I guess Sophie liked nicknames because she always called me Deena no matter how many times John, the kids, and I corrected her. It didn't bother me at all, because I always liked the name Deena.

I found out recently that Lisa had known Sophie for more than twenty years. Sophie rented an apartment that was on the second floor of Lisa's office building. When Sophie was evicted for leaving pots on and nearly burning the building down, Lisa felt bad for her. Lisa allowed Sophie to use her business mailing address and also stored some of Sophie's things in her office. Sophie confided a lot in Lisa, but not everything.

She once told her that she met a man at Burks Bend, now Casey's, and she fell in love with him. He called Sophie "Kitten," and she called him her "Puppy." Mc Ate was quite a drinker, and we don't know if he was all that interested in Sophie or if he was leading her on for some unknown reason. Sophie seemed to become obsessed with him and was always asking her friend Bob or Lisa for a ride to look for her Puppy or to see him. Both Lisa and Bob told me stories of driving up and down MacDade Boulevard, stopping at different bars and letting Sophie run in to see if her man was inside. Her behavior may have bordered on stalking.

I did the math in my head, something I admit I am not too good at, but I figured at that particular time, Sophie was in her late fifties. The thought of her having some fun made me smile. The thought of some sleazy guy taking advantage of a beautiful woman that may or may not have been capable of protecting herself made me so angry. The thought of her nearly burning apartment buildings down that long ago also concerned me. Perhaps I should be grateful and consider us lucky that I could never get her to operate the stove, the microwave, or the coffee pot.

~

I was surprised by the age of the woman behind the glass. She was definitely over the age of seventy. I thought I read somewhere that government employees had to retire at sixty-five. I guess that wasn't the case. She asked us for Sophie's birth certificate.

"This is all we have," I told the woman as I slipped Sophie's Medicaid card under the window. She shook her head.

"No, I need a birth certificate, a driver's license, or some kind of photo ID from the state," she said.

My first thought was, *Isn't Medicaid a state program?*

Anger was creeping in. I wanted to snap at her, but thankfully, I came to my senses quickly. I knew I only had mere seconds to win her over, so I gave it my best shot.

"Do you know her?" I asked the woman. "Do you know Sophie?" Not making eye contact with me, she shook her head yes. "Then please, just this one time, can you be compassionate and understand that I am only trying to help this woman. I have so many other things I would rather be doing, but God put her in front of me, and therefore, I have no other choice but to help her. Now here she is in front of you. Please, just help us. I will never say a word to anyone." The woman got up and walked away.

I thought, *Oh well, I blew it.*

She was getting the supervisor to tell me the answer is no or maybe even the security guard to throw us out of the building. He was already leery of us. A few minutes passed by. I started to get nervous. I wondered if we should just give up and leave. A few more minutes passed, and finally, the woman reappeared and slipped something into the tray under the window. I looked down and saw Sophie's social security card. Tears filled my eyes, and I got a lump in my throat. I told the woman she was an angel, and we left. I thanked God for that beautiful woman. I thought about how different the world would be if everyone used common sense and acted that kindly. It was also a lesson for me. Remaining calm in frustrating situations is not easy, but it sure increases your chances of being understood.

I was so happy that I used my own common sense and did not argue with that woman. Arguing was definitely what I wanted to do with her. I get that there are people that try to get away with things all the time. I am sure people try to get social security cards under someone else's name. I know that welfare fraud, Medicare fraud, and Medicaid fraud is rampant. I am all for ID laws, but every once in a while, it feels good to be given a common sense break. That was a kindness I intended to pay foreword tenfold.

I stopped at McDonald's to get Sophie a celebratory double cheeseburger. She took it apart and ate one of the patties and told me she wanted to save the other one for later. I was too happy to be upset with her at that moment.

Once I got her settled into the recliner, I got her a glass of apple juice and one of her new pills. I coaxed her and even tried bribing her to stop gagging and just swallow the darn pill. She was finally able to swallow it when I put it in applesauce and spooned it into her mouth. I put the TV on for her and went up into my office to write. It was so hard to concentrate.

I could not stop thinking about the lump on her back. I was so disappointed in and frustrated with that doctor. I wanted to believe him. I tried, but I knew he was wrong. I knew Sophie had cancer. I knew it the minute I felt it when I was washing her back.

She must be terrified. She took care of a close friend that died from cancer. I was pretty sure Sophie knew she had it too, and I was also sure there wasn't much of a chance of getting her to accept any kind of treatment. After seeing how frightened she was of a flu shot, I couldn't even imagine taking her for blood work, let alone any kind of biopsy or surgery. It was going to be tough, but there was no way I could possibly sit by and let this woman do nothing at all to help herself get well.

That doctor must have known how badly Sophie would fight any kind of treatment. Should I feel sorry for him or be furious with him? I was choosing to be furious. How could he just let her walk around with that big lump? I knew there was nothing he could do to force her to accept treatment. There was nothing I could do legally either, but I sure as hell was going to try everything I could think of to get her to cooperate.

I decided the doctor most likely tried to convince her to get treatment. I remembered how adamantly she told me she did not have cancer. It was all starting to make sense. I knew in my heart I had to try to talk her into accepting help. If she wouldn't listen to me, maybe she would listen to John.

John's mother had a friend that had a lump in her breast. She called John and asked him if he would drive her to the hospital and drive her back home the day of her biopsy. She had no family, other than a second or third cousin to speak of. She was never married and had no children. She spent the prime of her life caring for her mother. I felt sorry for her and tried to help her myself, but like Sophie, for some reason, this woman did not trust other women.

The night before her procedure, that woman called John and told him she decided not to have the surgery. She said she wasn't going to bother with any kind of treatment and she was going to give it all to God. She believed if it was his will, he would cure her. I was stunned. I couldn't imagine knowing I had that poison in my body and not wanting it out immediately.

Years later, that woman is still not only living but living on her own.

I also kept thinking about how kind the woman at the social security office was. She said she knew Sophie. I wondered how she knew her. I wished I had asked the woman for details, but I was afraid to push my luck with her. I considered going back one day soon when Sophie wasn't with me to see what the woman could tell me about Sophie's past. She wasn't old enough to have gone to school with Sophie. Maybe they were neighbors or their kids were friends. I couldn't wait to find out what she knew.

I wondered how much writing I would be able to get done before Soph started screaming for me to come down and tell her what was happening on her soap operas. She was the one who watched the shows 24-7, yet she expected me to know every detail of each story line. Maybe I was secretly hoping for a break from my writing. I was having a hard time concentrating.

The book I was writing at that time was the true story of the random road rage murder of my youngest brother, musician David Albert. I was at the part of the manuscript were I was adding how I felt during the trial process. It was emotional for me, to say the least. Sophie did not seem to understand how hard it was for me when I was writing. I couldn't seem to make her understand how much it took out of me physically and mentally. At other times though, she was extremely empathetic when I spoke of my brother and what happened to him. John often reminded me of how kind she was to him when his son died. She wasn't just being nice. It was more than that. John would say it was almost like she could feel what he was feeling. That made Sophie and me a lot alike because I definitely feel what others are feeling. I don't always like that ability. It can be exhausting.

Surprisingly that day, she let me work in piece for a few hours. I suspected she sensed how upset and how frightened I was for her. If I was sitting with her, she would see the fear in my face, and that would remind her how scared she was.

I wasn't looking forward to discussing the lump with John. I knew it was going to be heartbreaking news for him to hear. He loved Sophie so much.

17

Tell Them My Story

The entire time I was editing my first book, Sophie was begging me to write about her life.

"Tell them my story. My story is way better then that ugly old murder story," she would say. "I want you to tell *me* story."

She was worried that my writing the true story of my brother's murder and making the decision to use the real names of everyone that was involved in the crime and the story, including the murderers, their families, attorneys, judges, and my own family members, was dangerous. She was sure they were going to find out our address and come looking for us. I assured her over and over that the people I mentioned in the book would be the first people the police would look for if anything happened to me or my family.

I promised her I would tell the world her story one day and I would do my best to make sure people would read about everything that ever happened to her. I promised to write about everything the good and the bad. I laughed when she told me she definitely wanted me to use everyone's real name when I wrote her story.

"Sophie," I asked her, "is anyone from your life story going to come after us?"

She thought about it for a minute and said, "If they didn't want me to tell the story of what they did to me, then they shouldn't have done what they did." I would smile every time she said that because it is pretty much my motto.

How in the world was I going to get her to stay focused long enough? How would I ever be able to get entire stories from her, I wondered. It seemed she would go so far, and then she would freeze up and move onto another story. Whenever we had conversations, she would jump from one decade to another and then back again. She had her decades all mixed up. I needed to figure out a way to take notes and try to put her stories in some sort of chronological order. Then I would need to choose that one thing that happened to her in her life that changed her forever. That was going to be tough because every one of her stories could be the subject of an entire book.

While walking through CVS one day, I got the idea to have Sophie write down her own memories. I bought her a bunch of notebooks and pens. I have an obsession with any and all writing paraphernalia, so to say I was excited to pick this stuff out for Sophie was an understatement. I got her a handful of gel pens and fine-tip markers. I chose notebooks with pretty pictures of landscapes, puppies and kittens on the covers. I decided to pick up a few packs of regular old Bic pens that I could split with her. I could always use a few of those too. I wondered if she would know how to use tabs and highlighters and decided to get them anyway. If she didn't use them, I would. When I handed her the bag that of course included lots of writing snacks for her too, she got teary. It made me feel so good. I promised myself that I would tell her story and make her proud of the way it was told. Later that night, she asked me if I would mind getting her a few marble copybooks and pencils. That was our Sophie. She was thrilled when I returned with a bag full of marble copybooks and several packs of yellow number 2 pencils. I picked up the best but simple pencil sharpener I could find. I guessed she wouldn't use it, but I thought it was cute, and I could always sharpen her pencils for her.

It wasn't easy to get her motivated. I did my best to encourage her to write down whatever she thought people would be interested in knowing about her life. I thought it would keep her busy while I was busy with my own writing. Once she got started, it seemed like she was always writing in those notebooks. I was so curious to read what she was writing. She was extremely secretive about it and wouldn't let me see them. She told me I could see them when she finished. That made me smile because I don't like anyone reading what I'm writing until I was confident that it was the best it can possibly be, and that usually wasn't until I got to the final edit stage. I was hopeful when she asked for new copybooks.

Her friend Bob later told me that she talked about writing a book and telling her story for as long as he knew her. Occasionally, she would tell Bob, "They gonna pay for what they did to me 'cause me gonna tell all about it in a book."

Lisa told me Sophie also told her she wanted to either write a book on her own or she wanted to have someone write a book about her. Hearing this from the two of them, I knew I had to tell her story. There never really was a doubt I would write this book. It was just nice to know I wasn't the only one she told that it was what she wanted.

I was fascinated by her and heartbroken for her at the same time. What sin could she possibly have committed to be shunned by her entire family? I couldn't stop wondering what the answer was.

The fact was some people do seem to have an overabundance of misfortune, trauma, and pain in their lives. Sophie was definitely one of those people. People ask me all the time how I deal with all of the horrible things that have happened in my life, and my answer always is, for every bad thing that happens, I seem to have at least two blessings and more than a few miracles to feed my faith and to keep me hoping. I did not see Sophie having that balance ever in her life. Maybe she had glimmers of love and moments of peace and joy in her life, but overall, it was a life of pain. Maybe some of it was her own doing, but the more I realized how helpless she really was, I doubted most of the bad fortune that found her was her fault. I was determined to try to make up for that and do whatever I could to help her have joy in her life. I wanted her to have something fun to look forward to. I just needed to figure out what made her truly happy.

One morning while she was in the bathroom, I snuck one of the notebooks from the pocket of the recliner. What I found was page after page of phone numbers for stuff seen and only sold on TV. I quickly put the notebook back into the pocket of the chair and decided I should start writing my own notes about her life. I had to laugh. Sophie was always giving me money and asking me to order her that silly stuff from TV. She had me order two Snuggies for her, and she never used them. She said she did not want to get them dirty. The funniest thing she talked me into ordering for her was this hair removal system. It was a bunch of little colored sandpaper pads, and they were the size and shape of a dime. The instructions said to use your finger and move the pad in a circular motion over the hairy area. I could not stop laughing. Sophie insisted it would work. She was so mad at me for laughing. Of course, she wanted me to do it for her. There was no way I was going to stand there and rub her chin with that little patch, no way! She sat in the recliner and twirled that silly thing on her face for about ten minutes. That was the end of those ridiculous things. Into the side pocket of the recliner, they went never to be seen again. That did not stop her. Nearly every single day, she saw another product that she just had to have. I knew it was a huge waste of her money, and I felt guilty for indulging her and ordering these ridiculous products for her. I also knew that it was her money, and she had a right to do whatever she wanted with it. If it made her happy, then it was money well spent.

When I went to put the notebooks back into the pocket of the recliner, I noticed it seemed to be full, so I made a mental note to check into whatever the heck she had in there the next time that she went into the bathroom.

The pills her doctor gave her seemed to be working. Sophie seemed to be getting around better and complaining less. I was happy about that but also worried about that stupid lump. I decided to start loading her food up with garlic and onion. There was a lot being written about the research being done on antioxidants and how they do work to prevent and in some cases, to cure cancer. It couldn't hurt to try.

Since I was feeling a lot better, I knew the day was coming when I would have to go back to work. John and I were both concerned about leaving Sophie home alone with the dogs for so many hours during the day. I decided to call my boss at Home Instead Senior Care and asked her if it would be possible to do split shifts. She said absolutely, and it was no problem. I loved working for that company. I never worked for anyone that was so considerate of my time and needs. When they said they offered flexible schedules, they meant it. I hadn't realized how much I missed working.

We were worried, but there was no way around leaving Sophie home alone while we both worked. It didn't make any sense to hire someone to come in to look after her while I was out of the house looking after someone else. We prayed about it, often.

My first day back to work was with an elderly woman that lived about thirty-five minutes away in Broomall. It was a bit of a distance for me to travel for a four-hour shift, but I didn't want longer hours. I was too nervous about leaving Sophie and the dogs.

The client was a nice-enough woman, but oh my, her house smelled like cat urine. It was so thick I was sure I would be sick. It was not what you would expect in the area. It was a nice neighborhood, middle class, with swing sets in the backyards and children riding their bikes on the sidewalks. This house was also freezing cold. I made both of us a cup of tea and tried to find something reasonable to feed her. Her pantry was bare. I made her a scrambled egg. She asked me to feed her cat. I looked out into the yard and saw cat food cans all over the yard. They were scattered throughout the property like land mines.

Dear Lord, I thought, *she is attracting cats and who knows what other animals.*

How did the neighbors tolerate this mess? Maybe it was a neighbor that called and complained and that was why our service was called in to look after her. I debated whether I should clean up the yard or if I should save that chore for another day and spend the time getting to know the newest cat lady in my life.

There was an elderly woman in our neighborhood that did the same thing. I would take her to the grocery store occasionally. She always bought dozens of small cans of Fancy Feast, popped the tops, and scattered them throughout her yard. I tried to explain to her that the cats she was attracting had homes and most likely people that cared for them, so she was only causing them to eat too much and maybe even making them sick. She wasn't buying it, and it even made her angry with me.

One time, she was bitten badly. John had to take her to the hospital for rabies treatments. I did not think it was a cat that bit her. I was sure it was a squirrel or a raccoon. Her eyes were bad. Another time, I took her to the doctors because she had bites on her leg that became infected. That poor woman had no family other than a nephew that only checked on her when he needed something. I was relieved when she was forced to accept outside care in her home.

I located this new client's cat box and planned to clean it out, but to my complete surprise, it was already clean. The odor must have been from the cat spraying, or perhaps the laundry room door accidently was shut and the cat couldn't get in to use the litter box. I looked forward to cleaning the house. It was going to be a challenge to get rid of this smell, but I couldn't wait to give it a try.

That woman told the same ten-minute story over and over for four hours. She told me she had a brother that had five children and he lived in Virginia. She told me one of her nephews was killed in an accident while driving home after a visit with her. I didn't expect to hear such a heartbreaking story from her. When she told me his young children were in the car with him, I cried.

She also told me she had fallen in love with a young man from Media, Pennsylvania, which wasn't far from where we were, and for whatever reason, he married someone else. She remained friends with his sisters for many years. Those sisters were at times not the best of friends and left her out on occasion. It didn't take a scientist to realize they left her out when their brother and his wife were included. She told a specific story of the group planning to see a movie, and no one bothered to call to invite her. She was obviously holding onto that grudge for dear life, long after most of them passed away. I wondered if I should explain that it had to be because of their brother. I decided to let it go. I didn't know her well enough to know how she would react to any change in her story or her routine.

I was never so happy to be out in the cold when that shift was over. It felt good to breath in fresh, clean, cold air. It is so frightening to me to imagine how anyone could ever think it is okay to leave a woman like that home alone. She had no children and was never married, but she had plenty of nieces and nephews. They had to know she was completely out of her mind.

This was another one of those cases where a woman like this client if questioned would adamantly insist that she was okay and did not need anything from anyone. If someone truly wanted to help this woman, his or her hands would be tied. She has the right to decide if she is okay or not. The reality was, she was far from okay, and her neighbors and their children were being put at risk. Her house was disgusting, and she had no food. She was also freezing herself to death. As much as she thought she loved and was caring for her own cats and all of the cats in the neighborhood, the truth was, she was putting all of them at risk too.

After several shifts with that woman, I could no longer handle the odor. I felt so bad for the woman, but I couldn't stop thinking about getting some sort of infection or sickness from that odor. I would rather clean up poop, I thought. At least with poop, if you cleaned it up, you could eventually get rid of the smell. Be careful what you wish for, they say.

The first thing I saw when I arrived back home that day and opened my front door was papers strewn all over the living room. As I got closer, I realized it was Tastykake and Hershey bar wrappers along with shredded notebook and magazine pages. I asked Sophie what happened.

"Me was sleepin', and the dogs did it."

I asked her where they got all of the stuff.

"Me don't know," she said, looking down at the ground.

I started to panic as I picked the trash up. There must have been ten candy bar wrappers. I was quite sure chocolate was bad for dogs. They seemed to be okay. I asked Sophie how long ago this happened, and she had no idea.

"Why didn't you clean it up?" I asked her.

I knew that was a silly question as soon as I asked. She shrugged her shoulders. I knew they found all of this junk in the side pockets of that recliner. Dear Lord, there was crust from sandwiches, applesauce containers, and stuff I could not even identify. I blamed myself. I should have insisted she let me clean out those pockets. I needed to stop allowing or hoping she was capable of taking care of herself. I certainly could not ever trust her to care for the dogs. She loved them so much and they loved her, but I was so worried about all of them. I called the vet.

The vet said to keep a very close eye on the dogs. If they seemed lethargic, I needed to bring them over right away. I tried explaining to Sophie how important it was to watch the dogs. I told her she could no longer be allowed to keep any food in the pockets of her chair or on her side table. She moaned and complained but promised me she would be more careful.

At three in the morning, I woke up to the worst odor ever. I was scared to open my eyes. The dogs had the runs all over our bedroom. There was barely room to walk on the floor. It was that bad. I wanted to go downstairs and strangle Sophie. I wanted to go downstairs to get her and make her clean it all up. It took me two and a half hours to clean that mess up. I cried the entire time. I hated Sophie and the dogs the entire next day.

This situation was only going to get worse, I feared. I had no idea what to do. It did not make any sense to hire someone to come in and look after Sophie while I was out of the house looking after someone else. It made no sense that John and I should be responsible for such an expense either. I prayed for a solution.

Like an answer to my prayers, shortly after I went back to work at Home Instead Senior Care, John was laid off from his job. We joked that God had a sense of humor because we were both praying for an answer to the dilemma of what to do about Sophie while we were both at work. That was our answer. John would stay home and care for Sophie. Part of me wanted to laugh and part of me felt bad for him. It would be interesting to watch.

It was interesting for about a week. I was working extra hours out of the house and even more at home. Of course, John could not bathe Sophie, so that was something I had to do when I was home. I love my husband very much, but he is a lousy housekeeper and an even lousier cook. Between the two of them, I rarely had any time to write. I also never had a second to myself or had a chance to visit my kids or grandkids. It was nice that he tried, but the situation quickly became increasingly depressing for me.

John told me every night that he had no idea how I kept it together and was able to have so much patience with Sophie. He apologized for bringing her home and thanked me all the time for allowing him to bring her into our home. I knew in my heart there was no other choice for him but to bring her home, and I could never ever be angry with him for being the man of strong moral conviction that he worked so hard to become. He is a man that not only talks the talk but he walks the walk. How could I not support and admire that. How I would love to be the person that on nothing but pure blind faith put a homeless person in my car and brought them to my home.

That said, I could not wait for him to go back to work, but what on earth would we do with Sophie then? Was I going to have to hire a service like the one I worked for to come in and care for her the way I go out and care for elderly clients?

That wouldn't make much sense, but I was having a tough time coming up with any other solutions.

I knew there was no way I wanted to leave her in the house alone. It wouldn't be safe.

18

What Would You Do

I couldn't help but wonder back then what we would do if Sophie died in our house. The fact was, she would be dying in our house because she didn't go anywhere. I felt terrible at the time for even thinking about it, but being realistic, it was going to happen and we needed to be prepared. Would we be responsible for paying for her funeral? Did we even have the money on hand for something like that? How much does a funeral cost? During that time, I was so full of anxiety. I didn't even know how to go about researching what the protocol was for reporting a death in your home.

It would be so embarrassing to call someone and say, "Hello, and by the way, I was just wondering. What does one do if you wake up one morning and there is someone dead in their room that happens to be in your house? Do you call the police? Are you supposed to call an ambulance? When they arrived, what were you supposed to tell them?"

We didn't exactly have a complete medical history on her. I didn't even know if she had a middle name. Do they even ask for that type of information when someone is already deceased?

I considered if, when, and how I would ask Sophie if she wanted to be buried and where or would she prefer to be cremated? What a tough conversation to start, but one that I had no choice but to start. I asked her if she ever thought about where she would like to be buried.

"Me wanna be with my daddy."

I asked her where her father was buried, and she first said Darby. A few minutes later, she said he was buried in Sharon Hill.

I asked her who she could ask so she was sure. "Sophie, if something ever happened to you, I want to honor your wishes. I can't do that if I don't know what they are."

She shrugged me off. "I be fine," she said.

The next time I brought it up to her, she said she would like to be cremated and have her ashes sprinkled around in Glenolden. I didn't understand why she would want to be sprinkled in Glenolden. From the different stories she told me, it didn't seem like she was ever that happy in that town. Whenever I asked Sophie what was the happiest time of her life, she would tell me she has been the happiest and she has felt the safest since she had been with us. During another conversation, she told me she wanted her ashes put on the bar in Sam's saloon. She wanted to continue to remind people not to drink after she was gone. She said she had good memories from that bar.

When my ex-husband's mother passed away, the police called me. I went over to her house, and the police asked me to wait with her until the coroner arrived. My ex-husband lived on the other side of the state. I loved his mother, so I had no problem helping him out in that situation. I have to tell you, though, I sat there alone. Yes, the police left me alone with her for five hours, and it was tough. It was sad, emotional, and scary. At times, it seemed like the waiting would never end. When the coroner finally arrived and I questioned what took so long, he said it was a busy day. No apology from him for leaving me sitting in a kitchen with a dead loved one for five hours.

There was no way I wanted anything, anywhere, near as frightening as that ordeal was for me to happen with Sophie. I was clueless as to where to turn for help or even advice. I was wondering if we should see an attorney.

I suppose it takes a certain type of thick-skinned person to have a career as a coroner. I cannot help but respect the profession. The job has a long list of responsibilities. The number one responsibility is to determine the manner of and the cause of death. Sometimes, they can make a determination by gathering facts and other times, an autopsy must be performed. They are sometimes responsible for identifying remains. I would think one of the most difficult tasks would be to determine if an unnatural death was an unlawful killing or a suicide. In either of these cases, the evidence must be beyond a reasonable doubt.

Another difficult task for the coroner's office, which is an elected position, is the responsibility of maintaining death records and recording research, such as the leading causes of death in their jurisdiction.

In the United States, the top 15 leading causes of death, in order, are the following:

- Heart disease
- Cancer
- Stroke
- Chronic lung disease
- Accidents
- Alzheimer's
- Diabetes
- Flu/pneumonia

- Kidney disease

- Blood poisoning

- Suicide

- Liver disease

- Hypertension

- Parkinson's

- Homicide

The top 4 were not a surprise to me, and sadly, I must watch too much news because I assumed homicide would have been higher on the list. I was totally surprised by blood poisoning and flu/pneumonia. I was surprised by Alzheimer's too. I knew firsthand what a heartbreaking illness it was, but I hadn't realized it was such a deadly disease. Certainly, I never realized it was in the top 15.

With cancer the number two killer and with the billions and billions of dollars poured into research, I had so much trouble understanding why the treatment for the disease was still so barbaric. Was it simply because cancer is such a cash cow to the pharmaceuticals, the facilities, and the medical profession as a whole? It broke my heart to think that way, but I couldn't come up with any other reason. It was the same with mental health medications. Common sense would lead you to believe some sort of medication could be discovered that would have far fewer disastrous side effects.

I found out from Sophie's friend Bob that the friend she took care of, the one that had cancer, was the judge's wife. The same judge that she rented the apartment from until he sold it and she was evicted. The judge whose client was accused of discrimination. I asked Sophie what she did to take care of her friend.

"I made her tea and talked to her and stayed with her," she told me.

I tried but I could not picture Sophie cooking and cleaning or doing any kind of nursing chores. I could picture her sitting beside the woman just being there for her, to listen and to keep her company.

I could only imagine the reason the judge, his girlfriend (yes, he had one), and the kids threw Sophie out the moment the woman died had something to do with Sophie's lack of hygiene and housekeeping. Still they should have made sure she had a safe place to go. I'm sure she was a comfort to the woman in her last days. They should have helped her for that alone.

I started feeling angry again toward Sophie's family, especially her children. How dare they burden John and me with all this responsibility? We had our own children and grandchildren to take care of and be there for. My own parents had not even reached the stage of needing assistance yet. We had aunts and uncles to worry about and to help care for when they needed us. Who did these people think they were, and why did they think that they could just say to hell with her and all of her problems? She is no longer our responsibility.

Being angry with them didn't change a single thing other than my own blood pressure. Like worry, anger is nothing but a timesucker, and nothing productive could come from such a waste of time. We needed to solve the problem of what we were going to do if Sophie became physically disabled—or worse, she actually died in our home. I have always been a planner. I have always been the one that imagines the best and worst in every scenario and plans accordingly. John, on the other hand, is a fly-by-the-seat-of-your-pants kind of guy. If it happens, he deals with it then. One day at a time was his mantra. It is the one thing about him that drives me crazy, and my lack of spontaneity drives him nuts. We have both come through enough failed relationships to know and understand that life would be boring if we agreed on everything. We have so much more in common than we have differences, and common ground is the best place to start in order to solve any problem.

People would say to me, "I do not believe you put up with that woman and her mess for so long. You and your husband are out of your minds."

Statements like that made me so angry. They made me angry because partly it was true. I could not even believe I put up with this for so long. I honestly believed this woman would be in our home for one night. I foolishly believed that all sorts of money and housing assistance was collected for and given to the homeless people in our communities. I ignorantly believed shelters were safe places for the homeless among us to keep warm, have a hot meal, and to get a good night's sleep. What a rude awakening to realize they were nothing but magnets for criminals. I hoped her family was missing her and would step up to take care of her. I felt so foolish.

I also wondered why people like my husband would not think twice about bringing an elderly stranger into his home. Then there were the people like me that allowed their husbands to bring elderly homeless people home. What makes us so different that another man may not have even bent down that cold October night to help Sophie up onto her feet?

Another woman would have said, "Take her to the hospital and drop her off," or "Just leave her there on the sidewalk. She is not our responsibility."

Was there something wrong with us that we felt responsible for her? What would you do, honestly? I asked that question of everyone that asked me why we still had Sophie. Every single person I asked said that he or she would not have ever put Sophie in their car. They might have given her a few dollars, but that was all they would have done. They could not comprehend why we didn't simply put Sophie back on the street where John found her that night.

John is a disabled veteran, and every time we drive down Woodland Avenue toward the Philadelphia Veterans Hospital, we see dozens of homeless people walking in the middle of the busy road, carrying signs.

One says, "I am a veteran with a family, and I need help."

Another sign says, "I will work for food."

Some of these human beings are very young, which tells me they are veterans of recent conflicts. Others are clearly Vietnam era, and still others seem to be middle age. It bothers me. It's possible many aren't veterans at all. I've packed sandwiches and passed them out to them through the window of the car. There are a few of them that have dogs, so I have also handed out dog food and treats. I admit that I am scared of them. I imagine they might try to grab my arm or my purse, causing me to have an accident, or worse. John hands them money. I envy his lack of fear. Part of me wants to put them into the car and take them home with me. I know so much more now than I did when we first took Sophie in.

Most people, I would assume, simply drive by because they have no idea what to do. I wonder if the sight of these helpless souls tugs on anyone else's heartstrings the way they tug on mine. Especially this very young woman, she may be nineteen or twenty years old. She walks with a dog by her side and a guitar on her back. What did she do to deserve to be in such a frightening place? Was she addicted to drugs? Was she suffering from PTSD? Was she just a brat that didn't want to follow the rules and because of her stubbornness found herself out in the cold? I wanted to know all of their stories, but I couldn't do it again. I still didn't know Sophie's entire story. I had no time to try to figure out somebody else's story.

It was shocking to me to learn that the estimated number of homeless people in America is somewhere between 2.5 and 3.5 million. That is the population of some of our large cities. These numbers do not include the entire demographic of homeless that are doubled-up with family members or friends temporarily.

Research done by Dennis Culhane at the University of Pennsylvania, which is located across the street from the Philadelphia Veterans Hospital, followed thousands of homeless people in New York and found that on average, each of them used an average of forty thousand dollars a year in public services, such as increased health care costs. It would be so much less to provide an apartment and a social worker.

Approximately 26 percent of homeless people have a severe mental illness, and approximately 34 percent are chronic substance abuse users. That is more than half of the homeless population.

Most homeless families consist of a mother and at least two children and are identified as minorities. The woman are far less likely to have a mental illness or a substance abuse issue and are most likely to have fallen on a series of unfortunate events, such as the loss of a spouse or financial supporter, eviction, loss of job, or a lengthy illness.

Most families in homeless shelters stay for a period of six months or more.

Chronic health conditions among the homeless include at least 60 percent with dental problems, 50 percent with eye problems, 40 percent with chronic back pain, 30 percent battle diabetes, 30 percent heart disease, 20 percent depression, and 20 percent have had strokes. The dental conditions are no doubt due to the fact that Medicaid rarely covers any dental procedures other than removing teeth and providing poorly fitting dentures. We know this is true in Sophie's case. Medicaid doesn't provide much assistance for eyewear either.

It is heartbreaking that at least one and a half million of the chronic homeless people in America are children, and the most rapidly growing demographic of homeless are those aged sixty-two and older, most of them women. To me, this is completely unacceptable. These are the two most vulnerable demographics in the world, and here in the wealthiest, kindest, most giving country in the world, we allow the elderly and children to sleep on cold sidewalks, in frightening woods, or in crime-ridden shelters. We must do better for them.

Another fact that surprised me was that the homeless do not migrate for the opportunity of better services. Most of the chronic homeless are still in the general area of where they first became homeless. They stay in those areas because they are searching for work or have family in the area. I assumed because I always saw so many homeless people in Florida that they migrated there because of the weather. It was shocking to find out that Florida does indeed have a huge homeless population of Florida natives. Even more shocking was finding out that Florida is the most dangerous state for the homeless.

Fort Lauderdale, Florida, joined thirty other American cities and passed a number of ordinances to ban people from feeding the homeless in public areas, like parks. They also made it illegal to panhandle and leave your belongings unattended and strengthened laws forbidding urination and defecating outside. Residents and business owners pressured officials to create and enforce the ban to protect the neighborhood.

They went as far as insisting the police arrest ninety-year-old Arnold Abbott, not once but several times. Abbott spent more than twenty years feeding the homeless and was not deterred in the least by his arrests. He is a World War II veteran and was a civil rights activist. He started feeding the homeless to honor his wife's memory.

Fort Lauderdale mayor Jack Seiler said he thinks Abbott and others have good intentions, but the city can't discriminate in enforcing the law. He said it was passed to ensure that public places are open to everyone. He also stressed that the city was working with local charities to help serve the homeless through indoor feedings and programs that get them medical care and long-term help.

"The parks have just been overrun and were inaccessible to locals and businesses," Seiler said.

I understand the side of the residents and the businesses. Homeless people unfortunately can be dirty, and let's face it, dirty people can stink. Some look downright frightening. Some of them are mentally ill and have no filters when it comes to social situations. Some ask for money and/or food and can be relentless in not taking no for an answer. I do believe this type of panhandling should be illegal.

In our local shopping center parking lot a man approached me and said he was collecting cash to provide a Christmas tree for the shelter he lived in. He had a coffee can that was 3/4 of the way full of bills. For some reason I didn't believe him and it didn't matter because I had no cash on me. I told him that and he followed me across the parking lot, too close for comfort. He was not taking no for an answer. The man behind the counter at the dry cleaners insisted on walking me back to my car. I was grateful because the man scared me. I should have called the police.

Recently, in Philadelphia, a pregnant woman with a three— or four-year-old child stood on a corner in the city with a sign saying she was homeless. She received a lot of compassion and a pile of cash. And then someone filmed her getting into a BMW driven by a well-dressed man. The filming continued as she counted the money, and they drove away without securing the child in a safety seat. The first thing I thought when I heard this story was that perhaps the woman was a victim of human trafficking, but who knows, they haven't found her yet. For this reason and because of the fear induced by people like the man in the shopping center, I will never give cash to a homeless person—ever.

I like the idea of handing out *blessing bags*. These can be backpacks or bags filled with items, such as water bottles, granola bars, sandwiches, cookies, hairbrushes, combs, soap, hand sanitizer, sweatshirts, blankets, and just about any item that might be appreciated by someone living on the streets. Sophie loved the idea of handing these bags out too. She suggested we should put paper and pens and disposable cameras in them too.

I asked her why the cameras, and she said, "So when someone assaults them or they see a crime happening, they can take a picture."

The length of time a person stays homeless is diverse. Most report they have been homeless for at least six months, with many reporting it has been less than two years.

I was quite surprised to learn that most homeless people have and work regular jobs and receive very little if any government assistance. Then I remembered what happened with Sophie. To receive any kind of assistance, she had to have an address. Homeless people cannot get public assistance because they are homeless. We really do criminalize and penalize homeless people in this country.

~

It was painfully obvious that no one came to visit us anymore because of Sophie. Honestly, I could not blame them. Our house smelled terrible, and Sophie was mean and cranky and acted like a rude child most of the time. She tended to act out more when we had company in the house. I started feeling disconnected from our family and friends. It felt like our life had suddenly become boring, even stagnant. It felt like I was waiting for either something terrible or something wonderful to happen. Once whatever was going to happen happened and passed, we would be able to move on, to feel *normal* again.

So honestly, what would you do if your husband or wife brought home an eighty-year-old homeless person?

19

Placement

The change in Sophie was subtle at first. She was sitting in the recliner constantly again and not sleeping in her bed. She was seldom using the bathroom and seemed content to just sit in the chair and pee in her Depends. Getting her to bathe was an all-day struggle again. Getting her to do anything was an emotional battle for both of us. Not only was she exhausting me, it was painful to see her suffering.

John started to realize she was in a downward spiral. I saw the way he watched her and could see the sadness in his eyes. He rescued her. I believe he saved her life and he felt responsible for her life. I was terrified of what her loss would do to him. The loss of the dog and his parents in such a short span nearly put him over the edge. I knew Sophie was a replacement mom for John. She was someone he could be responsible for and protect. I did not want to take that away from him, but he was not the one taking care of or cleaning up after her.

One morning, I walked into her room to gather her bed linens so I could wash them. I saw something at the foot of the bed. When I saw that it was urine and feces, my head started to spin. Was this an act of defiance because I was insisting she sleep in her bed? Was it because I was encouraging her to get up and use the bathroom? I took a few minutes to calm down and asked Sophie why she did that to her pretty bed.

"Me didn't do it," was all she would say to me.

She refused to get out of the recliner and come into her room to look at the bed. I removed the sheets and put them in a pile on the floor with some dirty clothing. I picked up the tiny plastic trash can that sat between her nightstand and the bed. I noticed some tissue sticking out from under the bed. I got down on my hands and knees to look under the bed. I saw fifteen or twenty balled-up napkins. Literally scared, I reached for one and started to unravel it. The contents were approximately two tablespoons of petrified peas. I reached for another. This one smelled putrid. It held dried up scrambled eggs. Four or five of the little packages held the crust from her toast. It dawned on me that this was all food scraps that I had tossed into the garbage. Sophie was garbage can diving again. What was I going to do? I took a deep breath and tried not to cry. I was so angry that I had to clean this mess up. At the same time, my heart was breaking for her. I could not imagine how hungry she must have been at one or more times that she felt she had to take scraps of food from the trash can.

It was crushing to think she felt John and I would ever not provide her with food, let alone her favorite foods. I felt so sorry for her and so angry and frustrated with her at the same time. I took a few deep breaths and said a few prayers for patience and Sophie's mind and continued cleaning and sanitizing her room.

There was also a different look in her eyes these days. The look was glassy and far away. I had a feeling something happened, but I could not put my finger on exactly what it was. My uneducated guess was that Sophie suffered a stroke or a series of small strokes. I tried explaining to her why I thought we should take her to the hospital or at least to her doctor's office to be checked out. She loudly refused and swore she would run away.

"Me not goin' to no docker to be cut."

It was more than obvious that she was terrified of any type of surgery. She was also terrified of being left at a hospital. There was no doubt in my mind that that had happened to her more than once.

I could feel her spirit leaving. I felt we were beginning to lose her. Should I force her to go to the hospital? If I called 911, the EMTs would not take her to the hospital if she didn't want to go. There was no doubt in my mind she would loudly object. I struggled with what the right thing, and the ethical answer was in regards to her health. Somewhere along this journey with her, I was feeling like I lost myself.

Legally, we would have to go through the police and request something called a 302, which is a nickname used by law enforcement for involuntary placement in a mental health unit in a hospital or a psychiatric hospital. Anybody can request such a placement. The person making the request must also provide name and address of the proposed patient's guardian, spouse, parent, adult child, next of kin, or (if none of those exists) friend so that the hospital can fulfill its obligation to notify that person. That part was scary for me. Legally, would we be considered guardians? Also, if a person is taken to the hospital on a 302, it does not mean the patient has to accept any kind of medical intervention. The facility has the right to release the patient any time it feels the patient does not pose harm to himself or herself or others. They can only hold someone involuntarily for three days. If the facility believes the patient needs to be held further involuntarily, they must go to court and convince a judge. It was all so frustrating when all I wanted to do was to help someone who I believed was completely incapable of making a responsible decision for herself regarding her health care.

For the past two and a half years, our lives revolved around Sophie. If John and I wanted to go out to dinner, I had to prepare a dinner for her first. She would whine and beg us to stay home with her. We always invited her to come with us, but she would not leave the house. More often than not, we opted to stay home. It was not worth the trouble. When we traveled, it was a real fiasco. Not only did we have to arrange care for Sophie, we had to arrange a caretaker for the dogs. It was a full-time job getting out of the house, and a time-and-a-half job cleaning up when we got back home because of the odor and filth.

Maybe it was turning fifty or the PTSD or it was straight-up depression, but something had me feeling sorry for myself. I woke up in the morning feeling as if a concrete blanket was covering me. These feelings were not unfamiliar. In fact, they were very familiar feelings. They arrived like clockwork and had been doing so two years or so after every traumatic life experience or loss I had ever since my parents divorced when I was eleven years old. It was time for me to get serious about finding a new home for Sophie. I made a vow to myself that I would not get discouraged. I would put together a plan and refuse to take no for an answer.

I started back at square one. I called COSA. Once again, they took my information, and when no one called me back after three days, I called again. After several rounds of this and a very trying day with Sophie, I told the receptionist I was not going to hang up until she put someone on the phone that was capable of helping me. I felt bad for that receptionist, and I apologized to her repeatedly but I was adamant. I wanted to talk to someone that would not refer me to somebody else or some other agency. It needed to be someone that would tell me how to get Sophie out of my house and into a place that was safe, clean, and had people that would take good care of her. When a woman who said she was "in charge" finally appeared on the other end of the phone, I told myself to be mindful of my breathing, to stay calm, and to speak clearly. I started at the beginning and told her the whole story. She tried several times to interrupt me, and I sensed she was going to try to blow me off. That was not going to happen. That day, there was no way I was taking no for an answer.

The woman promised to help us. She said she would find a place for Sophie. I was afraid to believe her, but I had no choice. She promised to get back to me within a few days. *Right*, I thought. Part of me thought we would never hear from her again, but I decided to think positive. It worked because she called back two days later and said we could take Sophie to a place called Fair Acres. I said John and I wanted to visit the place first, tour where Sophie would be living, and talk to the staff. The woman seemed a bit put out by the request but said she would arrange for the visit. She called back and told us we had an appointment the following Friday to take a tour of the facility. In the meantime, I decided to do my own research.

In 1807, there was a group called the Director of the Poor. They opened a two-story building in Media, Pennsylvania, to house the chronically poor. The home also housed the insane, the mentally retarded, handicapped, orphans, widows, and deserted wives. Can you imagine? The facility eventually moved to a two-hundred-acre plot in Middletown, Delaware County, Pennsylvania—its current location. Conditions at the facility were not always good. In 1857, the residents were called inmates. I am thinking these were the types of facilities that drove Dorothea Dix to devote her life to reforming conditions for the mentally ill and the less fortunate. For one hundred years, the residents helped run the working farm by milking cows, planting fields, and canning.

Today Fair Acres is owned by the county of Delaware and consists of nineteen buildings, five of which are residential. Fair

Acres runs today strictly as a nursing home. Approximately one hundred and fifty of the nine hundred residents are under the age of sixty.

I was surprised to find the Delaware County Library system has its main office in one of the Fair Acres buildings. Also housed at the complex in a separate building is the juvenile correction center.

I checked for recent consumer complaints and any inspection failures. It seemed to me that Fair Acres was a better choice for Sophie than some of the other local homes. I worked in most of them at one time or another, and some of them are horrific. I was confident we were making the right choice for Sophie.

The day I had been hoping for was finally here, and you would think I would have been thrilled. I sometimes worked hard for this day. Some days I procrastinated. That stuff no longer mattered because the day was here now. Sophie was moving into a new home. Instead of feeling ecstatic, I was feeling guilty. The air in our home felt thick. John looked emotional, and we barely spoke that morning. I went downstairs to make us some breakfast. I was dreading seeing Sophie's face. I needed to keep it together for all of us.

For the first time in weeks, Sophie appeared with it cognitively. She was already dressed in the clothes I laid out for her the night before. In her eyes on that morning, I saw fear. The guilt was so overwhelming, but I forced a smile as I handed her a plate of scrambled eggs with a whole can of peas and two slices of bread with lots of butter. John was quiet too. I sensed his sadness. I hugged him and told him we were doing what was best for Sophie.

It was time to go. We had appointments set up with social workers and medical staff. I helped Sophie put her coat on, and John picked up her suitcase.

I looked at her and said, "Sophie, when you get well, your room will be here waiting for you."

I was not lying to her. I sort of knew she would never be back, but there was the possibility she could have had a urinary tract infection or some other infection that was making her act out. Perhaps they would be able to get her to have blood work done. My mind was wondering everywhere and anywhere but in this car. John had tears in his eyes.

I said again, "Sophie, please just do everything they tell you, and let them help you get well so you can come back home to us."

She said, "Me will."

John continued to be quiet. I knew he was fighting tears. John made the right turn that led to the gate for Fair Acres.

Sophie said faintly, "You's putting me in Fair Acres?"

I quickly put on the child locks for the car doors and answered her. I told her so much had changed, and it was the nicest place I could find. I promised her if she didn't like it, we would find another place or take her back home with us. I promised her we were not abandoning her.

She screamed, "God will punish you for this."

John and I both started to cry.

The building we were looking for was at the very back of the compound. That was comforting to me. There was a high fence surrounding the property, so if Sophie did happen to get out, she would have to walk pretty far to get to the main road.

When we pulled up to building number six, John and I were scared to get out of the car. What would we do if she ran? We both knew she would never get far. She was too sick, but still we were worried. I told John I would go inside and let them know we were there. I was hoping they would have someone who could help us get Sophie safely into the building. I was grateful they did have someone that was happy to come out and help us. Sophie was good, and we were able to get her inside the building safely.

Once inside, John went with Sophie. She always behaved much better for him. I went with the social worker assigned to Sophie's case to fill out more paperwork. She was a young woman who seemed quite disinterested that my heart was breaking. I felt like I was buying a car, not entrusting the life of a human being to her. Actually, it was much worse than buying a car. At least with new car buying, in the end, it would be exciting to drive the car home. There would be nothing exciting at the end of this process. There would just be worry.

I wondered how John was making out with his part of the intake process. After insisting the social worker provide me with the names and contact numbers of the people who would be responsible for Sophie's direct care, we went into the hall to wait for John and Sophie to join us. I chose a few brochures to glance at while I waited. I was annoyed with the social worker. It was obvious she did not want to engage in any sort of conversation. I had a feeling she would not be in this job position for long. She was visibly unhappy.

The ankle bracelet on Sophie stood out like a neon sign as she and John walked toward me in the hall. Sophie's demeanor seemed to have changed from anger to pure terror. John looked like he had been terrorized too.

Two women appeared in the hall and told us they were going to take us to Sophie's room. We got exactly what we wanted for her. She would be in a safe, wander-proof building. Her room was at the end of a long, roundabout hallway. The room had a huge picture window that looked out over a garden with a walking path, trees, and flowers. She had her own TV, and we made sure she would have the soap channel. She had a nice roommate. The poor woman was recovering from a broken hip, but she appeared to be mentally stable. The staff told us the woman's family visited often. Making sure Sophie continued to receive good care would be completely up to John and me. We would need to be committed to visiting regularly and overseeing her care.

John took Sophie's hand and walked her to the window. He told her they would have a great time walking through the garden. She seemed unimpressed. He moved on to the television. John patiently tried to show Sophie how this new remote worked, knowing that she would never remember how to use the thing. He decided to put the soap channel on for her. It was all she watched anyway. The cable package Fair Acres had did not include the soap channel. The aide assured us they would order it first thing in the morning. I doubted her. John promised Sophie he would be back the next day to make sure it was working. In the meantime, he found the station that showed old movies and left that on for her.

A nurse and a doctor came into the room to examine Sophie. The doctor immediately asked her where her teeth were. Sophie told him the story about how a dentist took them all out for no reason. He asked her if she wanted to see a dentist who could fit her for dentures. She said yes. He then told the nurse to write down that Sophie needed a soft diet. The nurse asked Sophie what her favorite things to eat were. John and I both answered for Sophie and said peas at the same time. We told her Sophie liked peas with all three of her meals, and we would be so happy if she could make that happen.

The doctor went on with the examination. He checked her eyes. They were fine. He wanted to see her walk, lift her arms, and to see how far she could bend. Then he had her sit back on the bed, and he began a physical exam. The first thing he noticed was the lump on her back.

"That needs to come out," he said quickly and looked over at me like, *Why has this not been taken care of before now?* The guilt was horrible. I said her primary doctor said it was nothing. I also told him I did not believe the primary doctor and I wanted Sophie to have a biopsy, but Sophie refused flat out. Sophie chimed in and said she needed to eat broccoli and garlic so she could cure her cancer. I looked at the aide and asked if she could add that to Sophie's diet. She said she could. The doctor dove right in again and asked Sophie if he could schedule the procedure to remove the lump.

Sophie screamed, "You people aren't gonna cut me."

I sat next to her and told her it was okay while John asked the doctor if they would continue trying gently to get her to agree to the surgery.

The rest of the exam went fairly well until he got to her toenails. I asked if they had a foot doctor on staff, and he said they did. Thankfully, Sophie agreed to let the doctor schedule a pedicure. I teased her about being in a resort. She smiled. The doctor finished the exam, and it was time for the room aides to introduce themselves.

A woman from another room kept wandering into Sophie's room and walking over to the window. She would stand there for a few minutes, turn around, and walk back out. About the tenth time she did this, she sat on one of the chairs in Sophie's room.

Sophie screamed, "Get her outta here."

The aides jumped up and directed the woman to her own room. They promised John and me they would do their best to keep that from happening.

The two young women led Sophie into the bathroom to show her around and to help her put her toiletries away. While they were in the bathroom, I stripped the bed and remade it with Sophie's own sheets, comforters, and pillows. I unpacked some photos that I put in frames for her of tiny hiney, the other kids, John and I, and of course, the dogs. I put Sophie's notebooks in her end table drawer along with some candy bars and small packs of snacks, like crackers and cookies. I asked the aide if Sophie could have some apple juice.

A young man from the kitchen arrived with a carton of apple juice and asked Sophie what she would like for lunch. After going over some choices, she decided on a grilled cheese sandwich with peas. The person said okay, and I wondered if he understood that she wanted the peas on the sandwich.

The aides continued their interview. They wanted to know if Sophie was able to shower alone, and I held nothing back and told them the truth.

"She will refuse to shower, and you will have to physically put her in there and wash her."

I looked at Sophie, and as sternly as I could, I told her she needed to listen to them when they told her it was time to shower. John told her too. She agreed she would not give the girls any trouble when it was time to shower. I gave them a few tips, like make sure they have everything within arm's reach ahead of time. I told them to also make sure her clothes were laid out ahead a time as well.

We all moved on to the closet area. There was plenty of space for all of Sophie's clothes, extra towels and blankets, and some of her personal items. I went back and forth on deciding whether to commit to doing Sophie's laundry or having Fair Acres take care of washing her clothes. Why was I having so much trouble releasing responsibilities to them?

John answered for me. "Just let them take care of the laundry."

I agreed. We hung her clothes and put her pajamas and socks in the drawers. Sophie said she wanted to lock her closet up so nobody could steal her clothes. The aides assured her the clothes would be fine. I could see the wheels turning in Sophie's mind, and I knew everything in that closet would be under her bed by morning. I felt guilty and a bit relieved that it would not be me convincing her to let me put it all back.

A woman came in and told us it was lunchtime, so we walked Sophie to the dining room and helped her find a spot. She changed seats three or four times but finally settled on one that gave her a good view of the large-screen TV.

We watched residents come into the dining room, some seemingly in great shape. We said hello to them and realized they were there because they were no longer here. Others in wheelchairs or walkers seemed sharp as tacks. I asked one nice woman if she would look out for Sophie for a few days and make sure she knew where everything was and did not get lost. That woman was so sweet and assured me she would also sit with Sophie at mealtime so she did not have to eat alone.

The aid arrived with Sophie's tray. There were no peas, and they gave her milk instead of apple juice. John was upset. He insisted they get her the juice. The poor girl explained they were out of peas and would have some for her the next day. Sophie barely ate half of her sandwich and told us she was ready to go back to her room.

John and I both knew the time to say good-bye was close. I was ready to get out of there, but at the same time, I felt so guilty and honestly, a lot afraid. I was afraid Sophie would act out, and they would not treat her right. I was afraid she would figure out a way to get out of there. I was afraid she would wake and be unfamiliar with her surroundings and fall. The aides assured us they would not let any of that stuff happen and that they would be hovering over Sophie for at least the first few days.

We hugged Sophie and promised her we would be back to see her the next day. She started to cry and so did we as we walked down the long hall without looking back. John reached for my hand and squeezed it tight. I was sobbing by the time we got to the front desk. The nurse in charge of the shift promised us she would personally look in on Sophie and she would call us if there were one ounce of trouble.

The ten-minute ride home seemed like it took hours. We were both quiet but teary.

Once we were home, I told John I wanted to put the recliner out for trash. He seriously asked me if we could have it cleaned. I just gave him the OCD look. We did offer to bring it to Sophie for her new room at Fair Acres but said she did not want it there. The two of us checked the side pockets of the chair. They were full of trash. We left it in there and hauled the chair to the curb. It had to be one of the saddest and yet the most freeing things I have ever done.

The stranger in our recliner became someone we loved. She became family, the dysfunctional kind of family member, like an eccentric aunt or crazy uncle. Seeing that chair on the curb made me feel like I did what I promised I would not do. Why did I feel like I put Sophie out on the curb with that chair?

I went into the kitchen and made us some lunch. We sat down on the big red sofa, turned the TV on, and ate our lunch quietly.

I looked over at John and said, "So this is the living room."

He laughed. It was so good to see him smile.

We called Fair Acres later that night and spoke with the floor supervisor. She told us Sophie was doing okay. She was quiet all evening and keeping to herself, but she was doing well. We were so relieved.

John visited the following morning. He brought a bag of cheeseburgers with him and passed them out to the residents. We thought it might help Sophie make friends. He watched TV with her for a while, and she told him she was doing okay but wanted to go home. He told her if she got well, she could come home. The next day, I visited. I framed some more photographs of the grandchildren, the dogs, and John and I, and brought them with me. I placed them on her windowsill. She seemed pleased. Sophie's roommate came over and admired the photos.

Then the roommate sat on Sophie's bed. Sophie told her to go sit on her own bed.

I turned the TV on for her and looked for the soap channel. It still wasn't available. When we went through the admission process, they told me it was available. I called the social worker. She apologized and promised she would arrange to have the upgrade made as soon as possible. She could not tell me how long it would take. I reminded her that I told her it was extremely important to us that Sophie have that channel and why. I was so frustrated and fought back tears. I did not want Sophie to see me upset. The aide explained to her they would have the TV fixed as soon as they could. In the meantime, I put on CBS for her and wrote down the times her shows aired. That social worker was not my favorite person the day of Sophie's admission, and again on that day, I was angry with her.

20

The Rainy Day Truth

My phone rang while I was on a shift for Home Instead. Normally, I would not answer the phone, but when I noticed the call was from Fair Acres, I became anxious. I feared a call telling me Sophie escaped and they could not find her or Sophie acted out so badly she was being expelled forever from the facility. Then there was the call I feared most of all. The call telling us Sophie took a turn for the worse or that she had passed away.

John and I both felt so strongly about not wanting Sophie to die alone. The staff promised to call us immediately if she took a turn for the worse.

The aide seemed upset and asked if I could stop by to see them at the nurse's station on my way home. My head was spinning with different scenarios. Sophie was getting kicked out, and I was going to have to take her back home with me. There was no doubt in my mind.

Oh well, I thought, *I guess that is just the way it is supposed to be.*

Wishing John was with me, several other scenarios played out in my mind as I drove to Fair Acres. My stomach sank as I passed through the guardhouse with no guard present and made a right turn and drove past several of the facility's residential buildings on the left. On the right was a vast green space with several smaller buildings that were pretty far off in the distance. This compound or campus reminded me of a military base. Each building was basic white with no distinct markings or color of any kind anywhere on them. Each building did have a number on the exterior that was difficult to see. I knew where Sophie's building number six was because of a section of fence at the edge of the parking lot on the corner separating the grass and the sidewalk that led to the double glass front door. Once inside those glass doors, there was another set of double doors that were kept locked at all times. There was a lockbox on the wall where we had to punch in a code that opened those doors. We called this building the safe neighborhood. All of the residents here were at risk if they were able to wander off into the community. There were a lot of woodlands in the area that could hamper a search. That was why Sophie was here. We would not be able to live with ourselves if Sophie wandered off and got lost.

When I arrived at the nurse's station that was located right in front of the elevator doors, an aide came out from behind the counter and asked me to take a walk with him. Once we rounded a corner and started walking down a long hallway, the aide told me Sophie tried to bribe him that morning into sneaking her out of the building. He handed me a crumpled one hundred dollars and said he took it because he didn't want her to be able to give it to anyone else. I didn't know if I should laugh or cry. He was visibly upset and didn't want to get in any trouble. I told him he did the right thing but said we needed to make sure she had not smuggled in any more money. I shook my head in disbelief. I was sure I checked everything so well when I packed for her.

She is something else, I thought. I was honestly relieved that she wasn't being evicted, so I couldn't help but smile.

Sophie appeared in the hallway and saw me talking with the aide. I recognized the way she was screwing up her face, and I froze.

She started screaming, "You get paid to put people in this place. You get people off the street with no homes and put them in here. How much they pay you to do that? You gonna rot in hell for that. God will punish you." She grabbed my arm, scratching it, and continued screaming at me, "She stole all my money. She has plastic surgery so you won't recognize her, but she's that same lady that brings all the people here to make money."

She just went on and on as I stood there, stunned. A nurse and several aides tried to calm her down. Residents quickly lined the hallway to try to get a glimpse of the cause of the disruption to their otherwise institutionally scheduled lives. I was so upset.

"Why are you always so mean to me, Sophie?" I asked her quietly. "What did I ever do to make you feel that way about me? I love you and just want you to be safe and comfortable."

Not happy that I couldn't stop crying, I thanked the aides and told them I had no idea why she was so upset with me. The nurse told me she thought it would be best if I left. She assured me they would get Sophie calmed down. I couldn't tell the nurse about the bribery situation because I did not want the aide to get in any trouble. I asked her to call John or me later and got back onto the elevator. I was shaking.

Sitting there in the parking lot in my car, I could not stop crying. I tried to figure out if I ever was cruel to Sophie. Did I deserve to be treated this way by her? Was I more worried about Sophie and her feelings, or was I just upset because I felt so embarrassed about being accused by her of cruelty in front of so many staff members? Did the staff believe her? What were they thinking? I believed all of the stories she told me. Why wouldn't they believe her? It was *so* clear to me now that Sophie was not always the victim she convinced me that she was. Did she ever really convince me that she was a victim, or is that just what I wanted to hear and believe to justify why I had a homeless stranger in my home for so long.

John was going to be so upset with her. He would be torn between being angry with her for upsetting me, feeling sorry for her, and feeling guilty because we could no longer take care of her in our home.

Once I calmed down, I realized Sophie was doing the only thing she knew how to do when it came to taking care of and protecting herself. When she felt cornered or trapped, she attacked whoever was standing in her path. We knew in our hearts we were doing what was best for her. Her safety and her health needed to be protected. I wish she realized that, but she wasn't capable of thinking clearly any longer. I wasn't convinced she was ever capable of thinking clearly.

I'm sure the staff understood the things she was saying to me were not true, but it was still embarrassing. Although I understood she was out of her mind, the outburst hurt my feelings, and I knew it would bother me for a long time.

At home, I sat on the big red sofa, staring out the large front window at the ugly bushes that formed a giant arch at the entrance to our front walkway. Sitting under the arch was Raymond, our neighbor's old orange cat. He was a friendly cat that John and I let in the house occasionally. He would walk around checking things out and let us scratch his belly and give him a few treats, and then he would be on his way. We hadn't let him in since we've had the dogs. He enjoyed sitting on the front porch, driving the dogs crazy, but he wanted nothing to do with coming into the house with them there. I remembered one day Sophie was sitting in the blue recliner. I was on the big red sofa, and Raymond was sitting on our front porch. I told Sophie I was going to let him in because I thought maybe he would get along with the dogs and they might like to play with him.

Sophie freaked out and started screaming, "Don't let that ugly cat in here. Me hate that stupid cat. He sits under that tree and waits till he can grab a bird and he bites its head off, eats it, and sits there waiting for another bird."

"That is ridiculous," I would tell her. "If he was doing that, we would see dead bird bones all over our front yard."

"He eats 'em," she insisted.

As I sat there that day after the confrontation at Fair Acres and all of the wondering I was doing over what truth Sophie told and what she told that wasn't true, I wondered what that cat was actually doing sitting under that tree. He was always looking up the tree. I never saw him kill a bird, but suddenly I knew that was exactly what he was up to. I started crying all over again.

Lance and Louie took turns sitting in my lap or at my feet. They knew I was upset, and now I felt bad that I was upsetting them. I started second-guessing the whole situation with Sophie. Should we have sucked it up and kept her here? That was ridiculous, I quickly told myself. It was only a matter of time before she would have wandered off, became lost, or worse. She was in no condition to be wandering the streets. We did what we thought was best for her, but did we have the right to make that decision? Why did we put ourselves in the situation where we were forced to make any kind of decision for Sophie's care?

I was still upset when John got home from work. When I told him what happened, he was angry. I told him I no longer wanted to visit Sophie on my own. He understood. We decided we would call the only two friends we knew she had, Bob and Lisa. We would tell them where she was and why. We had to make sure they understood that they could not take her out of the building under any circumstances no matter what she told them or offered them. We hoped they would go to Fair Acres to visit with her.

I wondered if she ever freaked out on anyone else the way she did with me. Maybe she snapped on Jim "E" Curtin's girlfriend or her own children. Her daughter Peaches did tell me her mother slapped her brother Billy across the face. John was able to reach her by phone, and he handed the phone to me.

At the time she told me, I almost laughed, thinking, *Is that a valid reason to banish someone, your own mother, to a life on the streets?*

Maybe there was more, a lot more to that story. I wanted to ask her, but I was so stunned I couldn't find the words. I decided I should just let it go. I believed deep down Sophie loved her daughter, but over the years she was with us, she made it abundantly clear how much she disliked and distrusted her own girl.

It was heartbreaking for me to even think about disliking one of my daughters that much—or worse, them hating me. It was difficult because my own mother was pretty darn mean to me. All I could think of was that I reminded her of my father or even herself. Maybe I reminded her of one of her sisters that deep down she didn't care for. Whatever the reason, I gave up trying to force her to love me and a funny thing happened. I was happier. Is that what happened with Peaches? Did she feel like there was nothing she could do to make her own mother love her, or was she a rotten daughter that stole her mother's boyfriend and money?

Part of me felt sorry for Billy, Sophie's oldest son. He seemed to have his life sorted out. What could it possibly be like for him knowing what happened to his mother over the course of her life. One of Sophie's friends, Diane, told me that Billy once told her Sophie was not an alcoholic. Diane thought Sophie enjoyed being involved with the twelve-step programs because she was obsessed with helping people.

"It was all she wanted to do. She would go into bars and pull people out and drag them to a meeting. If someone new came into a twelve-step meeting, Sophie stepped right up to help them. The way it is intended to work is the women are supposed to help the women and the men are supposed to help the men. Sophie preferred helping men and that upset a few people."

Diane said she heard from other people that Sophie wasn't an alcoholic. She didn't know what to believe.

"You would have no trouble believing she was an alcoholic because she had a bar fly look about her." She laughed. "She always wanted to look younger. She must have been in her fifties when I first met her, yet she still dressed as if she were in her twenties. She loved being around men and would get very jealous if a younger woman tried to give any attention to a man she was talking to, even if she was only interested in helping him."

I asked Diane if she felt that Sophie hated women.

Diane said, "She always liked me because I listened to her. She knew how much I appreciated the help and advice she gave me. She was always there for me when I needed her, and I tried to be there for her. She disliked any women that looked at or talked to any man she was interested in."

Diane told me that Sophie always looked out for her and told her what men to watch out for, which ones were married, who had a girlfriend, and who was plain no good. She said Sophie also got her involved in doing service and helping other people. Sophie loved Diane's daughter and loved taking pictures of the mother and daughter when they were together. Diane's daughter passed away not long ago.

"Just remembering how happy Sophie was when she saw us spending time together makes me smile now."

I wonder what it was about seeing the two of them that made Sophie happy. Did she miss her own daughter and wonder what it would be like to have a warm, friendly relationship like Diane had with her daughter? Did she think of her own mother and wonder what it would have been like to be loved unconditionally by her?

Diane was well aware of the fact that Sophie had mental health issues. She also realized she had some sort of developmental issues too but could not put her finger on exactly what it was. That said, she loved Sophie and was grateful to her because she was always there for her and for her daughter.

She had no idea what the issues were between Sophie and her family. She just knew that the family stopped including her when the family had a get-together and they stopped inviting her on holidays. She had no idea why. Diane did say that Sophie expressed to her how sad she was that she had no relationship with her sons. She also talked to her about her grandchildren and how much she missed them. This made me so sad because I asked her so many times about her grandchildren and she would never talk to me about them except for the one little girl, Frankie's daughter. Sophie never mentioned to Diane that she even had a daughter.

Sophie loved parties. Diane loved helping her decorate for twelve-step program dances. I asked her how much Sophie was able to do for herself at that time, and Diane said that Sophie could operate the coffee machines, sweep floors, and hang decorations. She said Sophie was obsessed with emptying ashtrays.

It was nice to hear there was a time when Sophie was able to operate appliances. It was also frustrating trying to figure out what happened to cause her to be helpless. John would tell you I happened and she was helpless because I did everything for her, but that wasn't it. She stayed with that man for a while, the one whose family insisted she leave because she wouldn't clean up after herself or keep herself clean. There was also the talk of her not being able to take care of her baby.

She did say that Sophie did not have a phone, and there was always something about Sophie that reminded her of a bag lady. She always carried so much stuff with her. She also walked everywhere. Diane did not believe Sophie was taking busses anywhere during the years she knew her. She was a proud woman, and even though she had a tough life and not much to show for it, she always held her head high.

Whether she was an alcoholic or not, the twelve-step programs gave her a purpose, a reason to keep a schedule, and she was a help to many, many people. Diane believed that and I agree with her.

"When we leave this world, we must leave having left a good impression on someone else's life. That is the Sophie we knew. The Sophie that helped so many lost souls."

Billy told John he would find facilities that would agree to take Sophie. He would take her there and get her settled in, and as soon as he left, she would run off. He said they repeated that until nobody was willing to help him find another place for her. Knowing how stubborn and persistent Sophie was, I had no trouble believing that she did indeed take off from these facilities. What I couldn't believe was that no one thought of placing her in a facility that had a no-wander zone.

I knew the term because my daughters worked at a facility called Mill Run in Bristol, PA. It was once a hospital, the Delaware Valley Hospital. My youngest daughter was born outside the emergency room there. The hospital was converted into a Sunrise Assisted Living Facility.

All of my daughters started their careers working in the dining room of that building while they were still in high school. Mill Run used ankle bracelets that would set off an alarm if someone wandered away from the building. When I first found out what the bracelets were for, I was kind of angry. I wondered why they couldn't just keep an eye on these fragile people. They were someone's loved ones. How hard could it be to keep track of a frail elderly person? I understood now after living with Sophie exactly how strong-willed and physically strong a frail-looking elderly person could actually be.

John continued to visit almost every day, sometimes bringing the dogs, always bringing cheeseburgers with him to share with the other residents. All of the residents and the staff enjoyed visits from Lance and Louie. I went with him on Sundays, sometimes bringing the kids along. Sophie seemed okay with me again, but I knew she remembered what happened. When John wasn't looking, she shot me some dirty looks. I understood how mentally ill and also how physically sick she was and the thought that she knew she was trapped in this place, with the fact sinking in that there was only one way she was leaving, was heartbreaking. I knew and understood all of that, but her attitude and lack of trust in me still deeply hurt my feelings.

John called Sophie's friend Bob again to let him know about the placement. He promised he would visit her often, and he also said he understood how important it was that he didn't take her outside no matter what she said to him, no matter how much she cried, begged, or yelled. John explained to him how sick she actually was. He told him about the cancer. Our biggest fear was Sophie walking out of Fair Acres and into the woods and not being able to find her. She would not be able to survive out there on her own in her condition.

Bob said he was going to let Sophie's son Billy know where she was and what her condition was. John asked him if he would have Billy call us before he visited his mother just so we could tell Sophie he was coming. We did not want to take the chance of a surprise visit causing Sophie to have another outburst, or worse.

For some reason, the thought of Sophie's kids visiting her suddenly upset me. She was *our* Sophie, and they had no business visiting her now. We took care of her. We loved her. We made sure she was safe. How dare they think they could walk into Fair Acres and claim her as their mother, like nothing bad ever happened between them. I thought all of these things and had these feelings, but I knew deep down in my heart that Sophie needed to see her children. She needed to make peace and say her good-byes. I needed to put my feelings aside again and do the right thing for Sophie.

John's conversation with Sophie's son Billy went well. Billy told him that he was appreciative of what we did for his mom. He said he tried many times to place her, but she always walked out of the facilities he placed her in, so he gave up, feeling like he was wasting everyone's time. The conversation with Sophie's daughter Peaches did not go well. I only spoke with her for a few minutes, and all she could tell me was that her mother smacked Billy across the face and that was unacceptable. She was defensive and rude. I am sure it is unacceptable to smack your adult son in the face, but isn't the punishment of sleeping on the sidewalk a bit much? I didn't understand her anger, but I also did not know her or anything about her, so her anger may have been justified. I just did not know why, and she wasn't offering any other reasons.

Jim Curtin, the Elvis impersonator, passed away while Sophie was in Fair Acres. Her friend Bob visited with her and gently gave her the news. Sophie was heartbroken. She confided in me long before this that she was in love with him and always had been.

"None of them other women know him like me do, and he loves me too. I know he does," she would say, looking at the floor.

After receiving this news from her friend Bob, Sophie never seemed to bounce back emotionally. She started to become more and more despondent, even with John. After not visiting her for a few weeks, I was stunned by the drastic difference in her appearance. She was getting so thin and appeared so frail. She looked so depressed. The attendant had her in a reclining wheelchair. Her eyes were empty. My heart stopped for a minute. How did this happen so fast? I tried to think of something that would cheer her up.

I asked her if she had any pictures of Jim Curtin. She quietly told me how she was his photographer and how she sold more tickets to his events than anybody else.

"Me loved him," she said. "That girl didn't take care of him, and he died. Me would give him garwic. Me would save him."

She went on to tell me that she believed the new girlfriend could possibly be lying to everyone. She believed Jim Curtin could still be alive. I asked her why she thought the girlfriend would want people to think he was dead.

"Because she wants him all to herself," she said.

I saw tears in her eyes, and I felt so bad for her. I put my hand on top of hers and told her I believed it was possible. I told her I would try to find out if the witch girlfriend was lying. I looked up at her eyes, hoping to see at least a tiny smile. There was none. I was still convinced that the woman did beat Sophie up at that storage facility and then took her Elvis collectables. I couldn't put my finger on why I believed it was true, but I did. I wished I could find a way to bring the woman to justice or at least out into the open and have her tell me why she did this to a helpless elderly woman.

Because John was seeing her more often, he had not noticed or was in denial of the changes in Sophie. It was also becoming more and more obvious that she was in extreme pain even while she was in a semi-sitting position. She was more comfortable lying in her bed. More and more often, that was where we were finding her.

I remembered the time I took her to a pain management facility. She had a standing prescription and occasionally went there for therapy on her hand, the one that the Elvis impersonator's girlfriend karate chopped. She whined during the entire therapy session. At that time, I went back and forth between feeling bad for her and wanting to scream at her and tell her to stop complaining. Now seeing her in this condition, I felt regret about the wanting to yell at her part. Here she was, sobbing in pain, and nobody seemed to be hearing her. I wanted to take her back home and take care of her again.

We wheeled her into the dining room, and I adjusted her chair to a more upright position. She cried out in pain, so I quickly adjusted it back to a reclining position. She pushed me away. The attendant put her lunch tray on the table. John asked him if he could get some peas.

"She was supposed to be given them for every single meal," he snapped.

On the tray were a grilled cheese sandwich, some vegetable soup, milk, and applesauce. I broke off a piece of the sandwich, dipped it in the soup, and put it up to Sophie's mouth. She turned her head, and I asked her to just try one bite. She refused. I tried giving her the soup. She ate a few mouthfuls of the soup and had a few sips of her milk.

"Me hurts." She started to writhe in pain, so we wheeled her back to her room and helped her into her bed.

John was visibly upset, and I had trouble holding back tears. We asked for the nurse. She told us Sophie was still refusing any medication for her pain. I kneeled down next to her bed and begged her to take something so she didn't have to hurt anymore. I asked her to take some Advil or some aspirin. She kept telling me no.

John looked at her and said "Sophie, you have to take something for your pain. It's not right that you are hurting so bad."

She looked at him and smiled and said, "Okay, John, me will take the medicine."

With that, the nurse hurried off to get the pills. When she got back, we asked for some apple juice. It wasn't easy, but we got her to swallow the pills. We were relieved that she would at least have a few hours of comfort.

It wasn't long after that visit that Sophie was placed in the care of hospice. The only thing about that news that was comforting to John and I was the fact that she would no longer be in pain. The goal of hospice is to keep you comfortable and improve your quality of life, while you are in the end stages of your life. Services are offered in your home, in a hospice center, or in a nursing facility. Their philosophy is the complete opposite of the usual medical community, which is to cure you in an institutional setting.

Hospice also provides medical services, emotional support, and spiritual resources for clients. The team members also provide help for family members and in our case, caregivers to manage the practical details and emotional challenges of caring for and preparing to lose a loved one.

During a visit, I sat on the edge of her bed. She was uncomfortable and moaning on and off. She was still being difficult when it came to taking medication. I looked in her eyes and told her I understood why she didn't like women and I told her I was sorry for every woman that ever hurt her. It is because of the lack of trust and sometimes the hatred we women feel for one another that keeps us covered in the shattered broken ceiling glass with only a glimmer of hope to get up there in the stars. We are so close, I told her.

"Sophie, did you know that it's women who run two-thirds of the world economy?"

She didn't answer, but I could tell she was present and paying attention.

"There are women that run some of the world's largest corporations. There are even women who run countries."

Her eyes were on mine, so I decided to keep talking softly. It seemed to be calming her down.

"Do you realize that if only we women could learn to agree to disagree, learned to debate effectively, learn to negotiate, and most of all, learned to love each other in spite of whatever our views might be or how different our lifestyles are, if we could only learn to examine what we have in common first and build on that, just imagine where we would be. Can you imagine a world without girl-on-girl crime of any kind?"

Sophie smiled. I didn't expect that and it warmed my heart.

"I can imagine that," Sophie said so softly I barely heard her. I kissed her head and told her to close her eyes and try to rest. "Keep imagining," I told her.

As relieved as we were that Sophie was finally comfortable and out of pain, we both knew that being in hospice care meant that the clock was ticking and we would not have our Sophie with us much longer. John was visiting nearly every day on his way to work. On most days, he visited again on his way home.

~

The rain was torrential that day. I was starting to see a pattern. Every year at this time, we had several rounds of downpours. It was spring's final release before relenting and allowing summer to take her place. This time of year is significant for John and me. We met for the first time and married in the spring.

During a difficult time in our young marriage, we decided to wear our wedding clothes and go to church together. When we pulled up to our house, it was raining so hard we couldn't open the car doors. We sat there in the car, talking to one another until we resolved our differences and realigned our hopes, dreams, and plans for the future. We got out of the car and made a run for the house. We were soaked through to our underwear but never happier.

That day, I had to make a run for the house again. It made me miss John, and knowing he would be at work until at least nine o'clock made me miss him even more. I hoped the rain would let up and the roads would dry because he took his motorcycle to work that day.

The rain always makes me think of my brother David. He loved rainy days. He was a mason contractor and when it rained, he would have the day off. On those days, he loved to spend time with his wife, infant son, and his guitar. I gave up wondering if I would ever stop missing him. It was clear I never would.

I changed my wet clothes and went about my usual routine of making the bed, doing a load of laundry, packing lunches and making coffee for the next day. The rain finally stopped, so I opened the front and back doors to let some fresh air circulate through the house.

John called to let me know he would be leaving work soon and he was planning to stop by for a brief visit with Sophie. I told him to be careful and to give Sophie my love.

Just as he was approaching the entrance to Fair Acres, John felt his cell phone vibrating. He pulled over. As he shut the ignition off, it started to rain hard. He dialed his voice mail. It was Ricky, Sophie's favorite nurse. He was crying. John's heart sank as Ricky's message went on to say that Sophie passed away peacefully.

I was hoping he made it to Fair Acres and was safely inside before the downpour started. The thought of him being on the road scared me. It's hard enough to drive a car in this stuff. On a Harley–Davidson, it was almost impossible and extremely dangerous.

I took one look at him as he walked through the front door, drenched, and knew something was horribly wrong.

"Sophie died," he sobbed.

We stood there, holding onto each other and sobbing for a long time. I got him some dry clothes to put on while he called Sophie's friend Bob and asked him to let Sophie's son Billy know.

Billy called John the following day and thanked John for everything he did for his mother. He said they were planning a service at her church and he would let us know the time and place. He never did.

John attended a memorial service at the twelve-step meeting hall where he first met Sophie. The hall was full, and everyone had a story to tell about how Sophie had helped them. I had no choice but to forgive them for not helping her when she needed them.

John often says we met Jesus and his name was Sophie. I believe him. She crossed John's path that night for many reasons. His heart was broken over the loss of his mother. Sophie filled that crack in his heart, and the thought of how proud his mother would be of him for helping Sophie helped him to look past her faults. She was also there to comfort him when he lost his father.

For a few months while Sophie was with us, the time shortly after my accident, we were having serious financial difficulties. It got so bad that a man came to our door to repossess John's motorcycle. He was devastated, and that repo man was not hearing or caring. Sophie scuttled off into her bedroom and reappeared with two fistfuls of five and ten dollar bills.

"Me has the money for that man," she told John proudly.

"No way, Sophie," he told her. "I am not taking your money."

"You have to, John. Me can't think about you not having your bike. Me will be sadder than you."

She had exactly five hundred dollars, and that was the exact number the repo man needed to leave the bike. That guy had no idea what was happening. He took the crumpled up bills and stomped off to his flatbed.

John said it all happened like a movie on slow motion. He said it felt like a miracle. We had no idea then and still have no idea today how she was able to come up with that money. We tried to repay her dozens of times, and she always refused vehemently.

We were having problems before Sophie arrived. We were working them out, but if Sophie wasn't there, we don't know what might have happened. It was a bit difficult to argue or fight with her there in our house. We were forced to speak kindly to one another at all times and to resolve our differences quickly and quietly. I am so grateful to her for that.

John quite often thanks me for allowing him to bring Sophie home that night. I answer him with a "Thank you." You really do never know what you are capable of doing until you have no other choice but to just do. Sophie taught me to be much more than nice. I have always been a "nice" person. She taught me to love, and that kindness is deeper than being nice. She has taught me to be kind to people that are less than deserving, and the people in my life that are hardest to love are the ones that need my love the most.

When I drive into Philadelphia now and see the homeless people lining the sides of the street, I don't see bums, drug addicts, or "crazy" people. I see Sophie, Jesus, and human beings that for whatever reason have ended up in this awful situation. I hand out tuna fish and peanut butter and jelly sandwiches, water bottles, and dog food. I do not hand out money. John does. Many cities have outlawed the feeding of homeless people on city property. Every time I read about or hear that, I cannot help but to remember the signs that say, "Please do not feed the animals."

The city's reason is the same. Feeding them will attract more. I understand that large numbers of homeless people can look frightening.

I doubt that John and I will ever take in another homeless person, but we will continue to feed them. We will also continue to try to convince our local politicians, community leaders, and churches to create simple programs that provide homes and social workers for the homeless. If we all simply suggest this program and maybe apply a little pressure in our own communities, I believe we can start a wave of change across the country.

There doesn't seem to be a day that goes by that Sophie doesn't cross our minds or come up in conversation. Whenever something strange happens in the house, like a shoe falls for no reason or we can't find something, we say Sophie is angry with us. When something good happens, we say Sophie is looking out for us. When it rains, we cry sad and happy tears.

We miss her.

Epilogue

The first Christmas after Sophie passed away was tough for John and me. We couldn't help but remember how she smiled when she came out of her room and saw the gifts for her under the tree. A package arrived. Not an unusual thing for that time of year. I opened the box and was confused to see picture frames, photographs, a charm, and a note. The note was from Sophie's friend Lisa. Looking at the picture of a younger beautiful Sophie, I started to cry. We couldn't thank Lisa enough for what we considered a message from Sophie, letting us know she missed us too but that she was okay.

A few months later, Home Instead Senior Care sent me to a new client in Glenolden. It was the first time they sent me to that area. The woman was in her nineties and having memory issues. She was not thrilled to have someone in her home invading her privacy. Within minutes, I realized how important it was for her to have someone to look after her. Her name was Gloria. Her home was small but immaculate.

"Do you do the cleaning yourself?" I asked her.

"Of course, I do," she snipped.

She did everything she could think of to ignore me, to get away from me. I continued to talk to her and tell her I just wanted to be her friend. I wanted her to think of me as a friend, a helper, and a companion. One day, I asked her to show me her garden. We went out into the backyard, and she told me how her husband chose the lot and built the house. She said they were just married and went on to raise three children in the house. The huge maple tree was planted more than fifty years ago, she said. We walked the perimeter, and she had a story for each of her many plantings. She was feisty and adorable, and it was hard not to fall in love with her. I noticed beads of sweat forming on her forehead and suggested we go back into the house. She didn't want to. She did agree to sit in the shade and allowed me to get a glass of ice tea for each of us.

I'm not sure why, but I started telling her the story of a homeless woman my husband brought home one night and how she stayed with us for more than two years.

Gloria's eyes got big, and she asked, "Was her name Sophie?"

I was stunned. She went on to tell me that Sophie went to her church and how her granddaughter Lisa had been helping Sophie for more than twenty-five years.

"Where is she now?"

My heart sank. After the initial thrill that I found someone else that knew Sophie, my heart sank, knowing that I now had to tell her Sophie passed away. Gloria was very sad, but I assured her that we took good care of Sophie and that she was reunited with her children before she died.

Lisa was shocked, to say the least, when she stopped by to visit her grandmother, like she did every day and saw me there. We both agreed there are no coincidences, and Sophie definitely had a hand in bringing us all together. Sophie would have loved to look after Lisa's grandmother. She did the next best thing. She sent me.

Lisa spent a few hours on the phone with me, answering my questions. She knew Sophie for more than twenty-five years. She allowed Sophie to use her business address so she could get mail, and she stored some of Sophie's belongings in her office.

Lisa was always there to give Sophie a ride or to let her use the phone and most importantly, to be a good friend to her. I felt bad that we never invited her to the house to see that Sophie was safe and happy. Why didn't we think of that while Sophie was alive? The only reason I can think of is that we were being so protective of her and didn't want anyone to hurt her ever again. It didn't help that Sophie wasn't that forthcoming with us and would never tell us who she trusted and would never tell us who her closest friends were. Lisa told me while she was cleaning out Sophie's storage unit that she came across a set of dentures. I couldn't help but laugh.

Sophie either misplaced them or she didn't like them. Lisa and I agreed to stay in touch. She also found numerous cards and gifts intended for her grandchildren. That made me cry. Where were those grandchildren?

Sophie's friend Bob agreed to talk with me to fill in some of the gaps. We never seemed to be able to make our schedules work to facilitate a meeting. We finally ended up talking on the phone for two hours. He shared everything he knew about Sophie and her life, and he told me she was furious with me for placing her in Fair Acres at first but then realized it was for the best. He admitted to being a bit angry with us too. He was upset that we kept Sophie sheltered at our house, and she didn't see any of her friends. I explained to him that I was always trying to take her to visit her friends, John offered all the time to take her, but she refused. I told him she wouldn't even go to visit her brother in the nursing home. I explained to him I didn't understand why she never wanted us to take her anywhere, but I assumed she was afraid we were going to leave her. I also told him we told her she could invite anyone over to our house that she wanted to, and she never wanted to invite anyone.

Bob was such a good friend to her over the years, and he was missing her too.

One night while sitting in a Panera Bread store on the other side of Philadelphia, more than an hour from where I live, with other members of a writing group, I was expressing how frustrating it was to find people to help me fill in the gaps of Sophie's story. A young woman, Alejandra, told me her new boyfriend lived in Glenolden. Jokingly, I asked her to call him and ask him if he knew Sophie. She did call him, and his answer was yes. He knew her husband and her son too. I made arrangements to meet with him, and he was able to fill in a gap and point me to the right neighborhood—Darby.

Jesus replied, "A man was going down from Jerusalem to Jericho, and he fell among robbers, who stripped him and beat him and departed, leaving him half dead. Now by chance a priest was going down that road, and when he saw him he passed by on the other side. So likewise a Levite, when he came to the place and saw him, passed by on the other side. But a Samaritan, as he journeyed, came to where he was, and when he saw him, he had compassion. He went to him and bound up his wounds, pouring on oil and wine. Then he set him on his own animal and brought him to an inn and took care of him.

—Luke 10:30–35

Sophie's Challenge

I challenge you to

- Perform one act of kindness for the homeless or the mentally ill, and if it feels good, make it a habit.

- Start a conversation at your dinner table on the topic of ending homelessness and then start the same conversation with a stranger.

- Send an e-mail to your town council, mayor, congressional representative, and senator and ask them what they are doing to end homelessness and how they feel about apartments and not jails or ERs for the homeless.

- Spread the challenge on social media. #sophieschallenge

doreenmcgettigan.com

Research Credits

Bio.com
Dennis Culhane, University of Pennsylvania
JFK Presidential Library
The Eunice Kennedy National Institute of Child Health Development
Philly.com

Made in the USA
Middletown, DE
16 March 2016